Game Design Deep Dive

In *Game Design Deep Dive: Trading and Collectible Card Games*, game design analyst Joshua Bycer is back to discuss the deck-building genre, from the original success of *Magic: The Gathering* to today's market with online card games like *Hearthstone* and *Gwent*. The design and philosophy of deck builders and tabletop games can be and have been applied to many genres.

- Looks at the history of popular tabletop card games and collectible card games
- Discusses how to design and balance your game with low numbers
- Examines the application of card-based design in other genres

Perfect for students and designers to learn about designing deck builders and card-based games.

Joshua Bycer is a game design critic with more than seven years of experience critically analyzing game design and the industry itself. In that time, through Game-Wisdom.com, he has interviewed hundreds of game developers and members of the industry about what it means to design video games.

T0139129

Game Design Deep Dive

Trading and Collectible Card Games

Joshua Bycer

CRC Press
Taylor & Francis Group
Boca Raton London New York

CRC Press is an imprint of the
Taylor & Francis Group, an **informa** business

Cover Design by Peggy Shu

First edition published 2024
by CRC Press
6000 Broken Sound Parkway NW, Suite 300, Boca Raton, FL 33487–2742

and by CRC Press
4 Park Square, Milton Park, Abingdon, Oxon, OX14 4RN

CRC Press is an imprint of Taylor & Francis Group, LLC

© 2024 Joshua Bycer

ISBN: 978-1-032-37083-5 (hbk)
ISBN: 978-1-032-37070-5 (pbk)
ISBN: 978-1-003-33521-4 (ebk)

DOI: 10.1201/9781003335214

Typeset in Minion
by Apex CoVantage, LLC

Contents

Preface

As the Game Design Deep Dive series continues, I am happy that I can continue talking about genres from a design perspective that are not really discussed along these lines. With CCGs and TCGs combined, this is one of the most popular and lucrative genres. Yet despite that, there is not a lot of information about the actual designing and balancing of these games for developers to look at.

This book focuses a lot on the design of these games, as the philosophy of table-top design is an essential skill for any game designer to learn. And despite the big names already in this space, the rise of deck-builder games has opened things up for new markets using these design philosophies. There are still plenty of genres left to cover, and if the audience here would like to suggest one for a future Deep Dive, please reach out.

Acknowledgments

For each Game Design Deep Dive, I run a donation incentive for people to donate to earn an acknowledgment in each one of my upcoming books. I would like to thank the following people for supporting my work while I was writing this book.

- Michael Berthaud
- Ben Bishop
- D.S.
- Jason Ellis
- Jake Everitt
- Thorn Falconeye
- Puppy Games
- Luke Hughes
- Adriaan Jansen
- Jonathan Ku
- Robert Leach
- Aron Linde
- Josh Mull
- NWDD
- Rey Obomsawin
- Janet Oblinger
- Onslaught
- David Pittman
- Pixel Play

Social Media: Social Media Contacts

- Email: gamewisdombusiness@gmail.com
- My YouTube channel where I post daily design videos and developer interview: youtube.com/c/game-wisdom
- Main site: Game-Wisdom.com
- Twitter: Twitter.com/GWBycer

Additional Books

If you enjoyed this entry and want to learn more about design, you can read my other works:

20 Essential Games to Study—A high-level look at 20 unique games whose design is worth studying for inspiration or for a historical look at the game industry.

Game Design Deep Dive: Platformers—The first entry in the Game Design Deep Dive series, which focuses on 2D and 3D platformer design. A top to bottom discussion of the history, mechanics, and design of the game industry's most recognizable and long-lasting genre.

Game Design Deep Dive: Roguelikes—The second entry in the Game Design Deep Dive series, which focuses on the rise and design of roguelike games. A look back at how the genre started, what makes the design unique, and an across-the-board discussion on how it has become the basis for new designs by modern developers.

Game Design Deep Dive: Horror—The third entry in the Game Design Deep Dive series, which examines the philosophy and psychology behind horror. Looking at the history of the genre, I explored what it means to create a scary game or use horror elements in any genre.

Game Design Deep Dive: F2P—The fourth entry in the Game Design Deep Dive series, which focuses on the mobile and live-service genre. Besides looking at the history and design of these games, I also talked about the ethical ramifications of their monetization systems.

All my books are available from major retailers and from Routledge.com directly.

1

What Is the Goal of *Game Design Deep Dive: Trading and Collectible Card Games?*

1.1 Introduction

For this entry in the Deep Dive series, I am turning to another immensely popular and profitable genre with **CCGs**, **TCGs**, and **deck builders**. This is a genre that those of you reading this have either become familiar with over the past couple of decades, or it is one you have never looked at (Figure 1.1). Still, the popularity of its design has transcended CCGs and tabletop games to become an incredibly popular form of gameplay to integrate into other genres.

Figure 1.1

Welcome to this deep dive. Maybe one of you will someday have a card game with as many cards as this.

DOI: 10.1201/9781003335214-1

Figure 1.2

I bet you were not expecting to see a first-person shooter in this book, but the reach of deck builders has gotten quite large.

Whether you want to work on a tabletop game or a video game, learning the lessons that have kept this genre alive and well will help you improve your own design skills.

1.2 What Is This Book About?

If you are hoping for the secrets to build the ultimate deck in your deck builder of choice, I am afraid this is the wrong book. I am going to be talking about the general history of popular TCGs and CCGs that have come to dominate the market.

An essential aspect of tabletop games and CCGs is understanding low-number-design philosophy, which has become the cornerstone of any kind of tabletop-styled game. Learning this will teach you about balancing games and the use of asymmetrical options that can be applied to multiple genres (Figure 1.2). Designing cards for any kind of gameplay is an important aspect that I will be going over. Over the 2010s, some games have made use of cards outside of a deck builder and have done things differently in terms of their design and made use of low-number design.

From that point, I am going to talk a lot about what balance means, and the philosophy here can be applied to any genre that makes use of a card or perk-based **system**. Part and parcel for the livelihood of these games is being able to grow them for months and years to come, and it's important to talk about how even the longest running games are still able to grow after years of support.

Even if you have no intention of building the next competitor to a game like *Hearthstone* or *Magic: The Gathering*, the lessons in this book can be applied to just straight deck builders and deck-building roguelikes, not to mention a tabletop game that makes use of cards. Thinking about games in this capacity will help you when it comes to creating gameplay and options that are more unique as opposed to being about higher numbers.

2

The Major Names of TCGs

2.1 Magic: The Gathering

For the TCG industry, *Magic: The Gathering* is recognized as the one that started it all (Figure 2.1). Richard Garfield is credited for creating the original concept. He approached Peter Adkison, the owner of Wizards of the Coast, in 1991 with a board game he had created called *RoboRally*. While Peter liked the idea, he really wanted a more compact game that people could play anywhere. The story goes that Richard had this concept for a game built around different magics that he worked on while he was younger that he altered to pitch the original concept of *Magic* to Peter, who saw the potential and money to be made.

After the team playtested and came up with the name *Magic: The Gathering*, the first public appearance of the game was in 1993 at Gen Con, the largest tabletop game convention in the US. The success and popularity of the game led to Wizards of the Coast receiving an investment of money to print its first set. The game was officially released that year, and the success was huge—selling out all the cards in the first printing.

Figure 2.1

Magic: The Gathering is the longest-running game and can now be played either in person or online.

DOI: 10.1201/9781003335214-2

Figure 2.2

Magic's different colors and their philosophies have been there since the beginning, and while dual-color cards have been created, there is very little possibility
of seeing a new color added.

From there, *Magic* only grew larger and larger as time went on. It had its first
world tournament in 1994, and the creators released multiple books about the
characters and world of the game, video games based on the game, and many new
expansions that added more cards and rules to it. While not every card is currently
playable, more than 20,000 different cards have been created for the game.

In 1999, Hasbro bought Wizards of the Coast for $325 million,[1] which it still
owns. At this point, it is hard to find an accurate value in terms of the money *Magic*
has earned since 1993, but given that it has brought in millions of dollars annually,
it is safe to assume that it has earned billions by now.

I will be discussing the design of TCGs/CCGs in general in the later chapters,
but I do want to touch on the unique design aspects of each game mentioned in
these earlier chapters. For *Magic*, a key aspect of its popularity is the many ways of
playing and building a deck. The core concept from the very beginning was to create different deck strategies based on the five colors of magic in the game—white,
red, blue, black, and green (Figure 2.2).

Each color represents a different element in the world and a different play style.
This provided an easy-to-understand guide for players when it comes to building
a deck and what color would fit how they wanted to play. Instead of having strict
rules for how decks could be built out of the factions, players could mix and match
the factions however they saw fit. The player builds their deck with land cards that
are color specific, which act as the resource system, creatures that can be played on
the board, and spells that provide a variety of effects.

By attacking, the first player who can do enough damage to reduce the opposing player to zero life points wins. When an attack is initiated, the defending player

Figure 2.3

Magic: The Gathering Arena is the latest attempt by Wizards of the Coast to create a dedicated online version of the game despite having failed several times in the past.

can assign creatures on their side to block the attackers and preserve their life points. If the defender does not have any creatures, or all the available creatures did not stop the attackers, then they will take damage directly. If a creature is not killed during combat, it will regain full health at the start of the next turn.

Another aspect of *Magic* are the varieties of card effects and rules associated with them. It is very common in the game for card abilities to break the normal rules of the game, or how cards interact with one another. This has only grown more complicated over the years with new expansions adding in new card types, rules, and even different ways of playing. This is an important aspect when it comes to card design that I will be returning to many times in this book.

As of writing this book in 2022, *Magic* shows no signs of stopping. An online version known as *Magic: The Gathering Arena* was released in 2018 (Figure 2.3).

2.2 Pokémon the Trading Card Game

Pokémon has been one of the most popular and profitable franchises in the game industry since its original release in Japan in 1996 by studio Game Freak. The game's concept was about exploring the world of Pokémon to capture and train the titular characters to fight against other players and be the top Pokémon trainer. At the time of the video game's release, the studio worked with another company affiliated with Nintendo, Creatures Inc., to develop a TCG version of *Pokémon* that was released in the same year (Figure 2.4). Both saw huge success in Japan that would then follow when they were released in the US in 1998. Originally, a com-

Figure 2.4

Pokémon, as a franchise, is one of the largest in the world and has been huge on TV with the animated series, multiple movies, the video games, and, of course, the trading card game.

pany called Media Factory handled the distribution of *Pokémon TCG* in Japan. When the game was brought to the US, Wizards of the Coast was the distributor. This partnership lasted until 2003, when The Pokémon Company stopped working with Wizards of the Coast and became the US distributor, and Media Factory would lose its rights for Japan later. Since then, *Pokémon* and all the games and licensing are controlled by The Pokémon Company, which is made up of Nintendo, Game Freak, and Creatures Inc.

In terms of revenue earned, much like *Magic*, it is very hard to find an exact number, but *Pokémon TCG* has also earned millions of dollars annually, not to mention the rest of the *Pokémon* franchise, and it's easy to assume that it has also earned billions in revenue by now.

Pokémon TCG's gameplay is easier to follow than *Magic*'s but still affords depth. Decks are made up of Pokémon cards for battling, items that can be used or equipped, and trainer cards that provide a variety of effects. Each player can only have one Pokémon at a time fighting, while the rest are on their bench (Figure 2.5). Like the video game, you can have evolved versions of Pokémon in your deck that you can use to evolve your Pokémon further, gaining more stats and new abilities. Every time a Pokémon is beaten, the winning player takes a card from their prize cards.

Energy is the game's resource and is represented by different elemental energy cards in a deck. One energy at a time is added to one Pokémon per turn to fuel their abilities. When a Pokémon is defeated, you also lose all the energy attached to it. To win, you must either defeat enough Pokémon to empty out

2. The Major Names of TCGs

Figure 2.5

Pokémon TCG's basic design has not changed since its inception and continues to be one of the most played trading card games.

your prize card pool, or the opponent has no Pokémon on their bench to swap in after losing a fight.

Over the years, the game has grown with special evolutions of Pokémon, unique types, different versions of the same Pokémon, and more. The game can be played online via *The Pokémon TCG Online* game that was first released in 2011 but has had updates and changes since. Besides that, new sets are still being developed, and tournaments are held around the world.

2.3 Yu-Gi-Oh!

The major TCGs that I am talking about in this chapter came from very different beginnings. *Yu-Gi-Oh!* was originally based off a **manga** created by Kazuki Taka-hashi in 1996. The name can be translated to "Game King" or "King of Games" and followed the adventures of a kid named Yugi, who played the in-universe ver-sion of *Yu-Gi-Oh!* called "Duel Monsters." The manga became popular enough to spawn an animated series, which further boosted awareness for the property (Figure 2.6). In 1999, the actual card game was created and published by Konami in Japan; it would be translated and shipped to the US market in 2002 along with the animated show.

Since then, Konami has retained control over *Yu-Gi-Oh!* and the property has been expanded with new animated series, mangas, movies, expansions, and mul-tiple video games on a variety of platforms. *Yu-Gi-Oh!* was one of the earlier TCGs to have an online version besides the physical one released in 2005. As of 2022, the latest online iteration is *Yu-Gi-Oh! Master Duel*, released on multiple platforms.

Figure 2.6

Yu-Gi-Oh!'s success in the US, just like *Pokémon*'s, was also helped by the success of an animated series.

Sadly, Kazuki passed away in 2022,[2] but the property is still going with new expansions and animated series.

Yu-Gi-Oh! is considered one of the highest-earning TCGs on the market, in no small part thanks to the varieties of products Konami has made for it, including limited-time collectors' packs and tins that I will discuss more in Section 5.2, and the money earned from the manga and animated shows (Figure 2.7). It is estimated that the game has earned more than $10 billion in its lifetime, not counting the revenue from the shows and other media, and has been one of the biggest moneymakers for Konami as a studio.

In terms of depth, *Yu-Gi-Oh!* would be closer to the depth of *Magic* as opposed to *Pokémon*. Decks are made up of a variety of cards, including monster cards, spell cards, and trap cards. Monsters are summoned to the field in either attack or defense mode, spell cards can be played to change the board state, and trap cards are used to counter specific strategies and situations and can be played on the opponent's turn.

Both players start with life points, and every monster card has an attack and defense stat. When a monster is in attack mode, its attack stat will be used during combat, and the defense stat is used when the card is played in defense. When a monster loses a fight in attack mode, the difference in points will be taken from the losing player's life point pool. If a player does not have any monsters on the field, they can be attacked directly for a lot of damage. The first player to reduce their opponent to zero life points wins (Figure 2.8).

Figure 2.7

Konami has released a variety of collectors' content for *Yu-Gi-Oh!* all around the world, with the rarest ones selling for hundreds of dollars even when the buyers don't know the cards in them.

Figure 2.8

Yu-Gi-Oh! Master Duel is the latest (as of 2022) in the many video game iterations of the game. Even the original Game Boy releases came with unique cards to try and drive up their value.

Figure 2.9

If there was a popular franchise in the 2000s, chances are there was a TCG for it. *Netrunner* stayed relevant thanks to its unique gameplay even though it has been years since an official expansion was released.

Since the original release, new expansions have raised the base stats for monster cards and introduced special summoning rules for unique monsters, multitudes of new spell and trap cards, and many more. While the basic rules for playing have not changed, expansions have greatly expanded the complexity of the game, and just like the other two games, there are still regular tournaments going on. For all three major games listed here, not only are people still playing them regularly, but they are also collecting and selling cards, which I will come back to in Section 5.3.

2.4 Where Are TCGs Today?

Just like any trend, once something becomes popular, there is a huge boom period of other studios trying to cash in. Throughout the rest of the '90s and into the 2000s, many different TCGs were released,[3] to the point that I could not list them all here. Just like the Massively Multiplayer Online Game (**MMOG**) trend of the 2000s, TCGs were developed around any recognizable property that was out at the time, from *Star Wars* to *Dragon Ball* to even *Harry Potter*. Many were published by Wizards of the Coast in the US.

One of the most recognizable and popular TCGs was *Netrunner*, which was also created by Richard Garfield in 1996 (Figure 2.9). Trading fantasy for cyberpunk, one player plays as a megacorporation while the other is a hacker trying to steal data. Unlike many other TCGs and CCGs, the different sides were not symmetrical in how they played. While the game is no longer in print, fans have been setting up ways of playing it digitally.

As of 2022, there are very few TCGs still in print besides the big three. Part of the reason for this is the huge cost and investment that goes into the genre, which I will be talking more about in Sections 5.4 and 9.1. There are still plenty of table-top games played via cards being released, but that is a different market and design compared to TCGs. The move to digital with CCGs is also a major aspect of how the market has shifted in the past few decades and is what I will be focusing on in Chapter 4. Today, many developers are skipping making a TCG in favor of CCGs, which are far cheaper to develop and produce. To help circumvent the physical cost of TCGs and tabletop games, Kickstarter and crowdfunding exploded over the 2010s to fund many smaller and self-published games.

There is a lot more history and design for each individual TCG that would fill books on their own. With that said, it is time to talk more generally about TCG game design.

Notes

1 https://money.cnn.com/1999/09/09/deals/hasbro/
2 https://nypost.com/2022/10/13/yu-gi-oh-creator-kazuki-takahashi-died-try-ing-to-save-woman-child/
3 https://en.wikipedia.org/wiki/List_of_collectible_card_games

3

What Is TCG Design?

3.1 The General Structure

Trading card games are usually played as 1v1 games, but there are variants and games that have supported more players at once. The goal of a TCG is to defeat your opponent using your cards before they can do the same to you.

TCGs can have different rules when it comes to the details I am going to talk about in this chapter, but the basics remain the same. Players will construct their decks using different kinds of cards (and I'll talk more about card design in Chapter 6) (Figure 3.1). The rules for what can and cannot be in a deck are different across the board. As an example, in *Magic*, decks cannot have more than four copies of nonland cards, and the minimum size of a deck is sixty.

One of the most debated aspects of TCGs and CCGs is the first-turn advantage. In Section 3.5, I am going to talk about what strategy and psychology mean in

Figure 3.1

Every TCG/CCG starts with rules for what is the play area, how to draw and play cards, and what you can do during a turn. From there, they can branch off in wildly different directions.

DOI: 10.1201/9781003335214-3

Figure 3.2

Resource systems are an important aspect of any TCG/CCG and can be as simple or as complicated as you want. *Magic* has added in special land cards with their own rules compared to the basic versions you see here.

these games, and that often starts with who gets to go first. Being able to control the flow of a match is a powerful advantage for the player that goes first—they get to place the first card or put down the first unit that the other player must respond to. Every TCG and CCG out there has different rules and advantages in place for whoever goes first or second. In the game *Hearthstone* (released in 2014 by Blizzard Entertainment), the player that goes second gets the card called "the coin" that they can use at any time to get 1 extra point of mana that they can use. There is also the option in CCGs that both players will play their cards at the same time each round so that there is no first-turn advantage, but only certain designs are set up for this.

Players start with a hand of cards at the beginning of the game and will draw, at minimum, one card, depending on the rules of the game, each turn. To play cards, each game has rules for what the player can put down on the board or how many cards they can play each turn. In *Yu-Gi-Oh!*, while you can play multiple spell and trap cards, you are only allowed to place, or "normal summon," one new monster on the board each turn, and that monster cannot be used to attack normally on the same turn. This is to give the opposing player a chance to produce an answer to that card. In a game like *Magic*, land cards are used as resources to play other cards, but *Hearthstone* simply has a mana pool that recharges each turn and dictates your options (Figure 3.2).

Every TCG and CCG is played turn by turn, with phases that dictate the available actions and responses. The most basic example would be this:

- Player's turn starts
- Player draws cards
- Player places cards
- Player uses cards
- Player ends turn

For more complicated games, turns can be further expanded on with different phases that allow either player to use different types of cards based on the situation at hand. A popular example is cards known as "trap cards" in *Yu-Gi-Oh!*. A trap card is designed to be played specifically if a certain condition is met by the opposing player during their phase (I will talk more about card design in Chapter 6). *Magic*'s version of this would be "instant" cards that can be played either during your turn phase or the opponent's. For many TCGs/CCGs built today, there will often be a rule for how long someone can take per turn. This is dependent on the complexity of the game and varies from game to game.

Another aspect of turns in these games is the order in which cards are "activated" during the play phase. When you have multiple cards from both players and different card types, all played on the same turn, it is important to set rules for the order in which these cards will be used. The reason is that many card combos work based on the order in which they are played on the board. Compounding that point, there are cards that will be played to explicitly counter the other player's strategy, and phases will be expanded to give players time to counterplay each other. A common methodology is that the order in which someone puts cards down during their turn will determine the order that said cards and their effects will be activated at the specified phase.

The most common win condition in a TCG/CCG is to attack the opposing player to reduce their life points—the first player to hit zero loses. However, one of the first lessons you should take away from this kind of design is that nothing is set in stone. Even though the big three TCGs I talked about in the previous chapter are the most popular, other games have done things differently and attracted respectable-sized audiences because of it. Another popular option we have seen over the 2010s are games in which cards add "points" to the field, and the player with the most points at the end of the game wins.

Trading card games are set up on either a playing mat with all the designated areas labeled or can be played anywhere if the players know this information already (Figure 3.3). The standard layout used will feature spaces for the following areas:

- The Player's Deck: the place where the player will keep their decks and draw cards from

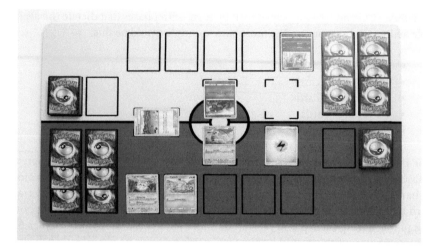

Figure 3.3

The play space in a TCG/CCG is one of those aspects that needs to be set during the development phase and before manufacturing begins. Outside of different art on the mat or board, designers will leave the gameplay-affecting areas alone.

- The Play Area: the actual space where cards are played, with clear limits on the number of cards that either player can have on their side at a time. Some games may have special areas to designate unique effects or where cards can go.
- The **Graveyard**: a space for where cards that are either used or defeated go and are considered no longer played, otherwise known as a discard pile. Many games do have card effects that can bring cards back into play or be used from it.

Once again, there are games with noticeable differences dependent on their rules and design, and even within the same game, there may be different formats that feature different board setups that I will return to in Section 9.2. A major aspect of TCGs/CCGs is acquiring more cards to play with, and that will be discussed at length in Chapter 5.

3.2 Low-Number-Design Philosophy

One of the biggest differences when we talk about the balance and design of table-top-style games versus video games is the use of low-number design. In previous Deep Dives, I have spoken a lot about **progression** and the use of scale—the player starts at level 1 doing ten points of damage; at level 50, they could be doing hundreds or thousands of points of damage.

Figure 3.4

Low-number design can be traced back to pen-and-paper games like *Dungeons and Dragons* and has been the cornerstone of tabletop, TCG/CCG, and many video games to this day.

A key appeal of tabletop games is the very fact that they should be playable without the need for any kind of computer or advanced math. This is where the philosophy of low-number design comes in—creating a game in which *every single point on a card matters* (Figure 3.4). If cards, by default, only have five points of health, going from 2 points of damage to 3 means that you can beat that card one turn earlier.

Even in games like *Yu-Gi-Oh!* in which card attack and defense values go into the thousands, there is no advanced math involved in how to play it—whoever has the higher-number card wins. From a design point of view, low-number philosophy keeps the ranges of values that need to be balanced far smaller than traditional games. In most **RPG**-style games, the character's stats will grow exponentially for as long as the player is finding new gear or leveling up their character. With low numbers, there is a hard limit on how high values can go for any attribute in the game. In turn, this provides a reliable framework for balance. Due to this framework, if a game does create cards that have higher stats than previous cards, this will alter the balance of the game going forward, so TCGs/CCGs designers need to weigh that decision carefully.

Low numbers also give you more freedom when it comes to designing a variety of skills, powers, etc. that the player can use. Because everything is balanced around a smaller number pool, skills that have unique utility or abilities tied to them are more interesting than just constantly raising an attack value. As a quick example, in *XCOM 2* (released by Firaxis in 2016), one of the early skills

Figure 3.5

In *XCOM 2*, any kind of action that cannot be dodged or could miss is inherently powerful. In design talks and interviews, Jake Solomon (the creative lead on the game) talked about being inspired by tabletop design when redesigning the *XCOM* experience.

you unlock for a class is the ability to send a drone out and do exactly 1 point of guaranteed damage. In other video games, 1 point would not mean much, as the player could easily be doing many times more than that with other attacks. Here, where the player must worry about the probability of hitting or missing, 1 guaranteed point can be huge for someone's strategy (Figure 3.5). There have been a lot of video games made over the years that borrow or directly copy low-number-design and tabletop rules for their systems. Any video game that uses one of the many editions of *Dungeons and Dragons* (originally released in 1974 by Gary Gygax and David Arneson) as their ruleset would be an example of this.

When it comes to deck builders, they may not be designed exclusively as tabletop games. While cards are initially balanced around low-number design, a major aspect of these games is the act of raising their value over the course of a run. For a game like *Slay the Spire* (released by Mega Crit Games in 2019), cards can be upgraded, and artifacts can be found that can increase the damage and potential of cards further. There is a greater focus on what the player can do each turn, as these games are usually played against a computer opponent. For more about the differences in design and balancing of deck builders, see Section 8.5.

The greater range of utility that comes from low-number design is part of the appeal of deck-building design and is a great segue into another unique aspect of this genre.

Figure 3.6

Card interactions and the interplay between them are what make a TCG/CCG interesting to play. The best games are never about just one card; they are about figuring out combinations of cards around which to create unique strategies.

3.3 Creating Card Dynamics

Due to cards being designed around low and easy-to-follow numbers, the depth and complexity of this genre comes in with the multitude of interactions and abilities between cards (Figure 3.6). How cards interact with one another can create all kinds of situations and strategies. Let us imagine that I am playing against an opponent with 2 health left who I am trying to finish off with a card:

Card: Fire blast

- Type—Spell
- Rarity—Common
- Cost—2 mana
- Action—Does 5 points of fire damage to the opponent

My opponent responds with this:

Card: Elemental Block

- Type—Field Spell
- Rarity—Uncommon
- Cost—3 Mana to play, 2 mana upkeep each turn
- Action—While this card is active on the field, all elemental damage is blocked

Figure 3.7

Advanced play in deck builders is about creating a unified strategy for your deck and filling it with cards to facilitate it. In this *Yu-Gi-Oh! Master Duel* example, summoning this card on the field will let me special summon another monster, which will then let me tribute summon for my remaining card.

Given these sets of cards, it sounds like my opponent is going to survive another turn and could counterattack me, but while I am attacking them with the spell card, I have this creature on the field:

Card: Devourer of Magic

- Type—Creature
- Rarity—Uncommon
- Cost—4 mana
- Stats—2 attack, 3 defense
- Effect—If any spell card is played while Devourer of Magic is on the field, do 2 points of damage to the opponent.

In the span of three cards, three different effects are used that individually do not do much, but here, they radically change the outcome of this match. For many TCG/CCGs that go on for years, they can have hundreds of special rules, modifiers, and potential synergies to explore (Figure 3.7). This can also lead to a huge nightmare when it comes to balancing and maintaining these games, something I will talk more about in Chapter 8. Beyond effects, cards can have **keywords** attached to them that define further properties and rules that go with them, and I will discuss this more in Section 6.2.

Figure 3.8

Having fixed classes or factions lets you firmly define the possible deck strategies and limitations of which cards can go together. In *Hearthstone,* each class has a fixed playstyle that is not shared between them.

There are no hard rules for designing the abilities and **mechanics** in your game, and the more creative options will provide depth for your players to enjoy. Making sure that everything is understandable both in physical and digital form is key to a successful game, and I will talk more about the **UI** design of cards in Section 6.1. A popular way of categorizing strategies is by using factions or classes (Figure 3.8). As mentioned, *Magic: The Gathering* features five elements distinguished by their color: blue, white, green, red, and black. Each color is broadly defined by different playstyles and mechanics that go with it. However, the game is also set up such that players are not limited to only one color's worth of cards and can mix but match them. Due to the potential of creating imbalanced decks, TCGs and CCGs will have different limitations on the amount and type of cards that can be in a single deck. I will discuss this more from a design standpoint in Section 8.1.

3.4 The Popularity of Deck Builders

Deck building as a game system has transcended the genre over the past decade, and its influenced can be seen in multiple genres that I will talk about in Chapter 7, but it does leave us with the question: what attracts people to deck builders in the first place?

Figure 3.9

Deck builders in all their many forms are about the creation and fine-tuning of one's deck so that while everyone is playing the same game, they are all using vastly different cards and strategies to win.

There are several answers to this question, and I will start with the simplest one: **IP** awareness. In my previous book, *Game Design Deep Dive: F2P*, I discussed how the marketability of popular IPs was used to attract fans to those games. For the deck builders that blew up, there are consumers who went to try them simply on name recognition alone. Just like mobile games and having collaborations, we have seen deck builders based off popular brands or the integration of them into games. *Magic: The Gathering* has seen sets featuring *Dungeons and Dragons*, *Godzilla*, and more over the years. As mentioned in the last chapter, there were many smaller TCGs made from popular movies and IPs at the time to attract those fans.

The second answer, and the one that this book focuses on, is the design and depth of deck builders (Figure 3.9). The best deck builders provide a wealth of **customization** and **personalization** options that players can spend months and even years to explore. In the previous section, I went over just a basic example of how different mechanics can interact with each other, but deck builders can feature complexities many times greater than that. Due to the ever-growing nature of these games with more cards and sets, a good deck builder is never "solved." It is not about having one faction or style of play be the absolute best but encouraging every style to be viable in its own way.

And even within each style, there are multiple variants based on the cards that people put into "their decks," and there is a reason I am using quotes here. Part of the attraction of games built on customization and personalization is the psychological motivator of building something that is uniquely theirs. Your deck that

Figure 3.10

The highest level of play in a TCG/CCG will be found at tournaments, such as the *Pokémon TCG* World Championships, where players will bring their best decks to try and be No. 1.

you built card by card because you enjoy them is fundamentally different from the cards that I enjoy in my deck. Some people can build an entire deck simply out of getting one card or finding a strategy they particularly like to use. This feeds into the competitive aspects of these games such that it is not just two players against each other, but two completely customized decks going at it to see which one is better (Figure 3.10).

When it comes to deck-building games, it is more about the challenge of creating strategies given that you cannot control what cards you are going to receive at any given time. Deck-building roguelikes are a key example of this, with every run having a wildly different deck created by the end of it.

The final aspect is one that designers have been marketing their games around since the start of trading cards: the collectability of these cards. Even the basic cards can feature impressive art designed to invoke a feeling in the player. However, the search for rarer cards has turned into a huge moneymaker for companies and collectors. There are collections of cards that are worth hundreds of thousands of dollars. While rarity often means more power, the successful TCGS also know that special versions of cards can mean big money to acquire them.

A standard of TCGs in this respect is having higher-rarity cards come with a "foil" or glossy finished to them; this makes the card's color shine differently based on the lighting. There is no gameplay-affecting value to foils, but the higher quality of the card combined with smaller printings means that people have spent a lot of

Figure 3.11

As I'll talk about later in this book, the aesthetics of cards can lead to huge money, especially if they are limited prints. Some of these cards pictured here sell for thousands of dollars.

money to get them (Figure 3.11). Foils are just the start, and much like designing these games, the only limit is the creativity and the money designers can spend on getting their cards printed. Advanced examples include holographic foils, using higher-quality card material to give a card a different feel, exclusive card art variants, and more. Even CCGs that lack a physical version can still make use of rarer versions with foils or special animations for their cards. The collectible drive to acquire all the cards has created a massive secondhand market with its own ecosystem that I will return to in Section 5.3.

3.5 The Mind Games of Cards

Like other card games before them, TCGs and CCGs feature a psychological aspect to playing them that is usually only seen in competitive multiplayer games. Your strategy for how you play your cards can oftentimes be more important than the cards in your deck. In the last section, I talked about how these games are about the depth of play and the options that players can exercise. Part of the mind game of play is that information is king—if I know that my opponent has absolutely no answer to my attack, then I can go all-in on this turn. The lack of information between players can lead to so many different plays and options (Figure 3.12). Sometimes, the best play is the worst from an optimization standpoint but the safest from a lack-of-information one.

Figure 3.12

Being able to read your opponent and their strategies based on their cards played is an essential skill for anyone who wants to play a TCG/CCG. That's how I managed to get a win in this example from *Marvel Snap*.

Figure 3.13

The longest-running games have become very daunting for new players to start learning, which is why game makers put out starter packs and premade decks to give newcomers something playable.

Even if my opponent's side of the board is empty, if they have a full hand of cards, any one of those cards could be the counter to my strategy. Or even better, none of those cards could stop me in any way, but I do not know that, and I must decide to take that risk. Therefore, from a utility standpoint, one of the best options a card can give you is the ability to look at your opponent's hand.

Due to the different ways you can play a game and the cards themselves, the strategies you can employ also add to the mind games. If for three turns in a row I keep playing white cards in *Magic: The Gathering*, one could assume that my deck is entirely built on white cards and the strategies that come with them. But just for fun, I could use a few red cards that the opposing player may never see coming until it is too late to respond. Many advanced players will study the different deck types and options available to try and figure out what strategy their opponent will use based on their starting cards.

This is also why having limits on what can go into a deck can create more decision-making when it comes to strategies and decks. In the game *Gwent* (developed by CD Projekt and released in 2017), the player has multiple limits on the type and size of their deck that I will come back to in Section 4.4.

Depending on the design of the game, different deck styles within each faction can also be used. Some decks could be designed around quickly getting out a lot of low-cost units designed to overwhelm the opponent. Another is all about countering the opponent and punishing them each time. For a game like *Magic*, there are countless hours of videos, articles, and design papers, all about the different methods and thought processes that go into a single match or to build a deck (Figure 3.13). Both players need to have a strategy not only for how they are going to play but also for deducing how the opposing player will respond.

Figure 3.14

While it won't be this simple, the beauty of TCG/CCG design is that you do not need to spend a lot to start prototyping rules and mechanics, and if your game is enjoyable to play using index cards with no art, then you are starting strong.

Uncertainty is the key aspect of this section and is something unique to TCGs and CCGs. If both players knew exactly what cards their opponent had, the entire match would be settled within the first turn based on knowing who had the stronger hand. In any game, all it can take is one card to completely upend the entire match.

3.6 How to Start Building a TCG/CCG

A huge focus of this book is going to be on the design and balancing of cards in a TCG/CCG, but all of that does not mean much if you do not have a basic structure and starting set. Before you even get one card printed, you must come up with how your game is played. Throughout this book, I am going to be discussing the flow and structure of popular CCGs/TCGs and card designs that you can draw inspiration from. This section's goal is to simply get you to start thinking about the foundation of your game before I get to the more complicated and design-heavy chapters in this book (Figure 3.14).

The first thing you need to figure out is how someone plays your game. This includes not only the rules of how to win but also the different phases that your game will have. Until you settle on the different actions someone can take during their turn, you will not be able to start creating any cards. You also need to decide how many cards someone starts with in their hand and how many can be drawn each turn. You will need to decide if your game has a resource system that limits the playing of cards each turn, and I will discuss this more in Section 8.2. As an

Figure 3.15

While *Magic: The Gathering* only launched with one original set, it was enough to show the varieties of play and has now grown to over 100 different sets, including expansions, and shows no signs of stopping.

exercise, think about the entire process of playing one match of your game—what can someone do each turn, how do players interact with each other, and how does someone win? From there, start thinking about how cards will be used to facilitate someone winning or be used to stop them. When it comes to the abilities and keywords on cards, there is an infinite number of ways you can design your cards that I will be discussing throughout this book.

The beauty of tabletop games is the very fact that you do not need much to start prototyping and producing a rough concept of your game. Paper prototyping has been a longstanding method for designers to test their designs and mechanics, regardless of making a digital or tabletop game. The play area will need to be figured out, and this is one aspect of TCGs/CCGs that, once established, is often set in stone outside of different game types.

Every TCG/CCG, in its first iteration, will be shipped with a base set of cards. Creating the rules, card designs, deck considerations, and more will be discussed throughout this book. For right now, your base set should be made up of more cards than your deck size limit, as there should be enough cards to produce different strategies and highlight the depth of your game (Figure 3.15). Your first set will define what consumers will expect as the base structure of your game and whether you have any unique factions that will enforce certain deck rules. While every TCG/CCG will grow with new cards, rules for playing them, mechanics, etc. over their life span, your first set should contain multiple types of cards, and it needs to attract people from the get-go if you hope to be able to grow the game for years to come. There is nothing wrong with sketching out additional expansion-set concepts and cards for the future during development, but you must settle on what will be included in your base set.

Once you have the basic game and card designs down, the next thing will be art. Card art means not only figuring out the style of your game, hiring artists, or doing it yourself but also deciding how you will distinguish rarity types and the amount of added work for rarer cards. For TCGs, this will come up again when it comes time to start getting cards and sets manufactured, which I will discuss in Section 5.4.

If you are building a CCG or having an online version of your TCG, there is further work that will have to be done with designing the UI and building the way for players to collect and compete digitally. Some TCG designers will hire a studio to create the digital **client** or do it themselves. Remember this for right now: just because you finish designing and getting a set printed does not mean that the work for developing a TCG/CCG is finished. In Section 8.6, I will be discussing why this is just the beginning.

4

The Arrival of CCGs

4.1 CCG vs. TCG

An argument that is close to the eternal "what is a roguelike versus roguelite" would be trying to settle on the differences between a CCG and a TCG. So far in this book, I have spoken about TCGs and the physical nature of them. To make things confusing, many long-running TCGs now have online CCG versions of their games.

To draw a line in the sand and define things for this book, I am going to categorize CCGs, TCGs, and deck builders as the following:

- TCG: A physical game played between players using cards that are acquired through buying sets and boosters; cards can be bought or sold on the secondhand market.
- CCG: A game that can be played similarly to a TCG but is done digitally, and there is no secondhand market between players allowing the exchange of money, but cards may be tradable (Figure 4.1). The game will allow you to buy boosters and sets only through the game itself.

Figure 4.1

Collectible card games provide the same complexities and depth of deck building but streamline the process of playing and collecting cards. Sometimes, it even changes the structure of the gameplay as *Gwent* has done.

DOI: 10.1201/9781003335214-4

Figure 4.2

Besides TCGs/CCGs, some tabletop games are played using cards based on a variety of properties, such as *The Binding of Isaac: Four Souls,* which was based off of the action roguelike *The Binding of Isaac.*

- Deck builder: A game that is about using cards to represent different tactics and can be attached to other game genres and designs.

Even with this breakdown, I have not spoken about tabletop games that are played with cards and managing a deck and hand (Figure 4.2). For this book, I am not going to be covering these games, as they are designed to be self-contained except for purchasing expansions and are different in design. However, the design philosophies when it comes to card balance and game design that make up the back half of this book can be applied to the genre.

To complicate matters even more, trying to accurately date the first example of a CCG can be tricky, as games like *Yu-Gi-Oh!* had CCG versions released on various platforms and an online game launched in 2005, and *Magic* has had multiple CCG and video game versions since its launch. For this reason, I am going to be covering original CCGs that were released either without a TCG version or with the CCG is the primary way to play. More about deck builders in general will appear in Chapter 7.

4.2 Hearthstone

Blizzard Entertainment has always been known as a studio that refines and iterates on popular genres, and its take on TCG gameplay with *Hearthstone* in 2014 is no exception. The game's concept came from Blizzard wanting to experiment

Figure 4.3

Hearthstone's success at streamlining TCG design made it one of the biggest CCGs on PC and mobile and would kickstart another period of studios trying to catch up to it with their own ideas.

with smaller projects compared to its megafranchises. Most of the game's development is credited to designers Ben Brode and Eric Dodds, but they were part of an internal team at Blizzard, known as Team 5, that would become responsible for the development and continued design of *Hearthstone*.

The original concept of the game was to create a TCG for the computer and streamline as many aspects of play as possible (Figure 4.3). This included designing cards with easy-to-follow rules, reducing the interactions and phases of each turn, having timers that restricted how long a turn could be, and other aspects. At the start, there were four kinds of cards in the game—creature cards with their own attack and health stats, spell cards that did something to the board, secret cards that were like the trap cards in *Yu-Gi-Oh!*, and weapon cards that could be equipped to heroes to let them attack directly.

Unlike the popular TCGs mentioned earlier, *Hearthstone*, from the very beginning, had asymmetrical design built into it with the use of classes. Each class was represented by a hero or major character from Blizzard's hit franchise, *Warcraft*. The class determined the kinds of strategy it could use, what cards were allowed to be in the decks, and a special "hero power" that could be used once per turn. I will discuss more about the impact of unique abilities and powers in Section 8.3. Another area in which *Hearthstone* innovated compared to other games at the time was trying to instill personality into the board itself. With TCGs being physical games, there was not much "flavor" to the act of playing the game.

Because it was digital, *Hearthstone* had animated details that could be interacted with while you were waiting for your turn; the different cards would animate

Figure 4.4

Hearthstone would popularize this concept of making the act of playing livelier with cards literally launching attacks and featuring an interactive board that made watching the game more exciting.

and attack in unique ways and much more (Figure 4.4). To stand out from TCGs, *Hearthstone* turned its expansion sets into bonus challenges in which players could go up against unique scenarios to win free cards from the new set. The game became very popular for people both to get in a few matches when they wanted to and to play for hours on end.

The structure for online play and integrating mobile game practices like daily quests and premium currency in CCGs were at the forefront of *Hearthstone*. Of the newer CCGs, *Hearthstone* was the first to have a mobile version, which further broadened its appeal. The combination of Blizzard's reputation and the easiness of play made it a huge hit. Like with the other games, it is hard to give an accurate number regarding the money earned, but it had earned tens of millions of dollars a month for eight years at the time of writing this book.

As for the general play of *Hearthstone*, players take turns playing cards and summoning creatures to the board, with creatures normally unable to attack the same turn. Mana acts as the game's resource and is refilled each turn. With every turn that goes by, the mana pool is increased by 1 up to a limit of 10. When creatures attack, they will lose health based on the attack stat of the opposing card. When a card runs out of health, it is defeated. Players can only take damage if a spell or creature targets their hero directly or via the use of a secondary effect or keyword. Since the release, the game has added additional ways of playing, expansion sets with new card rules and keywords, and more (Figure 4.5).

The game has seen many ups and downs regarding card balance and general play. It is far harder to gain rarer cards in *Hearthstone* due to how booster packs

Figure 4.5

Every new expansion for *Hearthstone* has come with new cards that fit a specific theme while changing the state of the game.

were designed, with very low chances of pulling epic and legendary cards (the two highest rarity types). Even though the team has changed over the years, it is still one of the more popular CCGs on the market.

4.3 *Shadowverse*

In *Game Design Deep Dive: F2P*, I spoke a lot about how the mobile market changed in the 2010s. A major factor that led to what I consider third-generation mobile games was developers looking to new genres and designs to apply Free-to-play (F2P) gameplay to. A lot of these games would end up coming from outside the United States, and *Shadowverse* by Cygames was one of the earlier examples being released in 2016 (Figure 4.6). As with the games discussed in this chapter, *Shadowverse* was designed to compete in the CCG space against the likes of *Hearthstone*.

Based on its own original world, *Shadowverse*, like *Hearthstone*, has a class-based system when it comes to deck rules, and mana is restored and increased each turn. Decks may only have cards of the same class and neutral cards in them. The rule for decks is that you can only have three copies of any card, and decks must be 40 cards long. Where *Shadowverse* plays differently compared to other CCGs is with the mechanic of "evolving" cards. Each player gets evolution points at the start of the match; the player that goes first gets 2, and the one who goes second gets 3. On turn four for the second player (and turn five for the first player), you may spend 1 evolution point a turn to evolve a card to a higher form. When this is done, the card gains higher stats and may change its properties as well (Figure 4.7).

Figure 4.6

Shadowverse was one of many CCGs released to compete with *Hearthstone*, and it managed to succeed thanks to its own original universe and take on card dynamics.

Figure 4.7

The mechanic of evolving cards over play isn't something we see a lot outside of *Pokémon*, but *Shadowverse* turns it into an interesting but limited strategy.

This system allows someone to change the trajectory of a match by upgrading a card at the right time, while the limited number of points means that the decision about which card to upgrade is a hard one.

Figure 4.8

Gwent's success came out of nowhere for the developers, but the game has since carved out its own space in the CCG market.

Since the game's release, it has earned more than $100 million in the US but is played far more in Japan. It is also the only CCG mentioned in this chapter that has an anime series based on it, which was released in 2020.

4.4 Gwent

The game industry is full of cases in which nobody could have predicted the success of a character or system, and *Gwent* is one of those examples. As a game, *Gwent* has gone through three completely different iterations of its design. The first one was in the game *The Witcher 3: Wild Hunt*, released in 2015 by CD Projekt and it was simply a minigame that players could play with the various characters in the world (Figure 4.8). Its popularity convinced developer and publisher CD Projekt to create a standalone competitive version of it, with that one entering an open beta in 2017. By this point, CD Projekt's game-development side got a slightly different name and is now known as CD Projekt Red. In 2018, the game hit 1.0 following another redesign and was officially released on multiple platforms. That version remains current to this day.

In terms of **monetization**, players can buy new character portraits, booster packs that come in the form of "kegs," buying both premium currency and cosmetic currency for cards and buying access to their story-driven expansions for more cards for now. Cards can come either in a standard form with a still image or in an animated form that is rarer with no gameplay differences between the

Figure 4.9

Deck strategies are different across the board between factions and even within the faction itself. This card represents the theme of Nilfgaard's faction of impacting both their side and the opponent's side of the board.

two. As for revenue, due to the multiple revisions, it is harder to gauge how much money the game has earned over its lifetime at this point, but it is safe to say that it is in the tens of millions of dollars as of 2022.

For the gameplay, *Gwent* is based off *The Witcher*, a property written by Andrzej Sapkowski and translated to game form by CD Projekt. Unlike the other TCGs/CCGs featured in this book, *Gwent* was not originally designed as a competitive game but as something players could play against AI opponents. This led to it having a different structure and pacing compared to other games.

In the game, matches are played based on three rounds, with players taking turns putting cards onto two different parts of the field, representing the "melee" row and the "range" row (this was originally three in the previous iterations). Every nonspell card in the game has a point value associated with it that is added to the player's point score for that round. Many cards have specific keywords and abilities that activate based on where they are placed, what cards are next to them, or what the opponent has (Figure 4.9). In turn, they can raise their point value or their ally's or lower an opponent's card value.

A round is over when both players pass on their respective turns, and you automatically pass when you do not play a card on your turn. After each round, the cards on the board are sent to the graveyard (with a few exceptions), and players draw a few additional cards to start the next round. Because a match is played out over three rounds, card advantage is important, and players do their best to preserve it from round to round. If you play every card in your hand on round one

Figure 4.10

Gwent's different take on card designs and their match structure has made it stand out from a lot of other CCGs.

to win it, you will be far behind the opponent for rounds two and three. To win a match in *Gwent*, a player must win two out of the three rounds by having more points than their opponent.

Deck limits have also changed over the different iterations of the game. In the current version of the game, decks must have, at minimum, 25 cards, and players can have two copies of bronze cards and only one copy each of gold cards. Every faction is locked to only cards from its respective faction and those from the "neutral" faction. A new attribute was added with a "provision" rating, which every card in the game comes with—the more powerful the card, the more provision attached to it. Decks now have a provision limit of 150 points on top of the minimum and maximum limits on individual cards.

Another aspect unique to *Gwent* is that each faction has different "leaders" that can be assigned to a deck. The factions have multiple leaders that can be chosen for an additional provision cost. The leaders come with a unique power that can be activated throughout the match, and the impact and number of times it can be used is different for each leader.

Gwent's different take on game design has earned it a following as the CCG you typically play if you are not a fan of the designs of the other major names in the market (Figure 4.10). In terms of its expansions, the game does something like *Hearthstone* by releasing story-driven expansions that players can buy and complete to unlock the new cards besides buying kegs and opening them for additional cards. Even though *Gwent* did have a surprising early success, the game has

Figure 4.11

The number of CCG-styled games to come from the indie space is extensive, but very few managed to survive for the long term. While you can still play *Haxity* here, it is no longer being supported.

dropped considerably in terms of its player base, with the current plan, as of early 2023, to end future development of cards by the end of 2024.

4.5 A Brief History of CCGs

The 2010s brought with them a wide range of CCGs and games that made use of card-based mechanics. I will be discussing the latter in Chapter 7, but this was the first decade for video games as internet access became cheaper and more standardized around the world. The successes of games like *Hearthstone* started another period in which developers were trying to make the next hit CCG.

Unlike with the MMOG bust of the 2000s, developers this time were not just trying to copy *Hearthstone* but to create a new CCG experience to rival it (Figure 4.11). While none of these games did manage to achieve the same financial success as the top ones mentioned in this chapter, the best ones did manage to cultivate a healthy and supportive fan base.

In 2016, *Duelyst* by Counterplay Games launched on Steam after a successful Kickstarter in 2014. The lead design came from Keith Lee, who first worked for Blizzard. The concept here was to take a CCG and combine it with a tactical strategy game focusing on unit-based combat. Players built their decks out of minions and spell cards that could be played and choosing a general that acted as the leader. Each general had their own stats and special abilities and belonged to one of the game's factions. The object was to defeat the opponent's general before they did the same to you. *Duelyst* focused more on the units on the board compared to other

Figure 4.12

Duelyst was one of the stronger CCGs from the indie community for a time but is now unplayable now that the servers have been turned off. Plans are to bring it back with the fan-supported *Duelyst 2,* seen here.

CCGs, as positioning mattered for stopping enemies from attacking a general and setting up special attacks and spell ranges (Figure 4.12). Players could buy new cards and cosmetics using real money and the game's currency. While the game proved to be successful as a different take compared to other titles and was picked up by the publisher Bandai Namco in 2017, it eventually died. Servers for the game were shut off in 2020 due to a declining player base. However, the game will not be dead for long. At the time of writing, *Duelyst 2* was released with the blessing of Counterplay Games by Dream Sloth Games and is being designed and balanced by the hardcore fans of the game.

In 2013, the Kickstarter for the game *Faeria* by Abrakem succeeded, with the game entering early access in 2016 and officially launching in 2017. The game combined CCG design with strategy gameplay of moving units around a board. Player decks at launch included creatures and spell cards, with new rules and keywords added through expansions. Players needed to build out their land from their starting area to capture mana points on the map to fuel their cards, and many cards could only be used if the player had a prerequisite number of land cards for its color. Units could block other units, and the board in each game would be dependent on what land cards were played where (Figure 4.13). Unlike a lot of other TCGs/CCGs, *Faeria* launched with a sizable amount of single-player content, with puzzle challenges and fighting against a variety of AI opponents. The game boasted that players could unlock cards without needing to spend on booster packs. The player earns battle chests through play, and the player will never get

Figure 4.13

Faeria's unique gameplay can be tied to its "living board" and how the state and structure of it change with every game based on how players build out.

duplicate cards. Even though active development of new content has stopped, the game had four expansions of new cards, and its online mode is still accessible and being played. As a funny aside, Abrakem would go on to work with Richard Garfield on a deck-building roguelike called *Roguebook*, which was released in 2021.

2017 also saw Bethesda Softworks, the makers of the famous *The Elder Scrolls* series, getting into the CCG space with *The Elder Scrolls: Legends*. The game was originally launched exclusively on Bethesda's own digital platform, Bethesda.net, and would later come to Steam and other platforms. Unlike with the other games mentioned in this section, a lot of people compared *Legends* to *Hearthstone* in terms of style and play. *Legends* tried to stand out with having two lanes to play cards in and cards based on different colors to build decks out of (Figure 4.14). The game drew from different games in *The Elder Scrolls* franchise to build expansions around. Development of the game started with the studio Dire Wolf Digital, but it was replaced by Sparkypants Studio in 2018. Unfortunately, the game never managed to stand out enough to attract new players, and development of new content ended in 2019.

In 2018, Valve entered the CCG market with a partnership with Richard Garfield to create *Artifact* based on its popular **MOBA** *DOTA 2* (originally released in 2013). Unlike the other games, *Artifact* was launched with a retail cost of $20 and was not free to play. Cards could be put up on Steam's marketplace and bought and sold, with Valve getting a cut of every transaction. When the game launched, it lacked some of the basic features of other games, and there was no way to get new booster packs through play; everything could only be bought with real money, including entry to the game's tournament mode.

4. The Arrival of CCGs

Figure 4.14

The Elder Scrolls: Legends just didn't do enough compared to other CCGs to stand out, and an overhaul wasn't enough to keep this game going.

The game design was unique and attempted to model the three-lane structure of a MOBA into three different play fields. The objective is to destroy two of the three towers in the lanes before your opponent does the same. Each play field has its own mana pool, and there were no limits for deck or hand sizes (Figure 4.15). Unlike other CCGs, card attacks and even where creature cards will show each turn are random, with the player able to earn gold from killing enemy cards to buy cards once each round is over. The different factions were represented by colors, and you can only play spell cards if you have a hero in the lane with the same color.

Unfortunately for Valve, despite creating an original concept, the higher investment at launch and the players not responding to the random elements led to *Artifact* spiraling down. Even with Valve releasing major updates and trying to save the game, it never recovered, and Richard left the project in 2019. In 2021, Valve cancelled development on any new content for the game, made the final iteration free, and shut off marketplace support.

The other popular MOBA on the market is, of course, *League of Legends* by Riot Games (released in 2009), a game I discussed in *Game Design Deep Dive: F2P*. In 2020, Riot decided to try to beat *Artifact* and *DOTA 2* at their own game and released a CCG based on *LOL* with *Legends of Runeterra*. While it is based on the MOBA, *Legends of Runeterra* does not go for the same multilane approach but changes things by having players alternate between attack and defense each turn. Every champion has different conditions to level up, which can change their abilities and raise their stats (Figure 4.16). While the game has not earned as much compared to the largest examples, it is still being played and is more popular than *Artifact*. I estimate that it has earned more than $10 million so far.

Figure 4.15

Artifact had the opposite problem—it was very different from other CCGs on the market, which made it harder to start playing. Being the only game that you had to buy at retail to play didn't help grow its audience, and this will go down in history as one of Valve's rare absolute failures.

Figure 4.16

Legends of Runeterra's "level up" system for cards based on specific conditions is an interesting way to design a deck around. Despite being based on a MOBA, the game doesn't try to take those elements in the same way that *Artifact* attempted to.

Figure 4.17

Marvel Snap is currently trying to out-*Hearthstone Hearthstone* with a game that is even quicker and easier to start learning and playing. As of writing this in 2022, it is still unknown just how successful the game is going to be.

While it's still too soon to say if it will succeed—literally, as I was finishing writing this book in 2022—a new CCG called *Marvel Snap* was released by Second Dinner Studios, which was founded by Ben Brode after he left Blizzard and the *Hearthstone* team. The game is designed to be both an entry point for newcomers to TCGs/CCGs and something for Marvel fans to play. Deck sizes are capped at 12, and matches are only played up to six turns. To win, players take turns placing cards to try to control three randomly chosen locations; whoever has the highest combined point total in a location controls it. At the end of turn six, the player who controls at least two out of the three wins the match (Figure 4.17). At this time, it is still too early to say where it will be in the future in terms of content and support.

In addition to the games mentioned in this section, there were other CCGs and a variety of deck builders that would use cards in their own ways, which I will talk about in Section 7.1

5

How Monetization Works

5.1 Micro- (and Multiple) Transactions

In my last Deep Dive, I said that covering monetization systems in these books was going to be a rare occurrence, and yet here we are doing it back to back. Both CCGs and TCG are examples of **live-service** games. For more information about the philosophy and approach of live service, you can find that in *Game Design Deep Dive: F2P*. For the present purpose, a live-service game is one that is meant to be continually supported and updated for months, and oftentimes years, to come (Figure 5.1).

Unlike with the games I talked about in the last book, the monetization options and systems of TCG/CCGs have become standardized. The main monetization of TCGs would obviously be the cards themselves, and I will focus on that in the next section. Just like with any popular IP, additional products can always be produced for sale, including binders, sleeves for cards, guidebooks, custom playmats, and even more paraphernalia. Much like the mobile games I talked about, IPs that become big enough can enter other markets; *Magic: The Gathering* has had novels about the lore released since the '90s, and *Yu-Gi-Oh!* has the aforementioned multiple TV shows, manga, and movies.

Because CCGs are digital, they do align themselves closer to mobile games with their monetization. It is common for CCGs to have purchases for new boosters and expansion sets like TCGs. Where they differ is in oftentimes making use of regular and **premium currency** options (Figure 5.2). While players can buy premium currency for real money, it can also be earned through play or completing daily and seasonal challenges. Many CCGs will have specific tournaments and modes that require premium currency to enter but can pay out with free booster packs and/or premium currency to the top players.

Instead of opening boosters to get foil versions of cards, these games either save them for their rarest tiers or allow players to spend currency to get animated/foil versions of cards (Figure 5.3). Unlike TCGs, in which players can pull and own multiple copies of cards, CCGs will limit a player's collection to the max number that can fit into a deck. When a player pulls multiple copies beyond what they can put in their deck, they are typically converted or "milled" into a special resource. If the player gets enough of this resource, they could trade it in to unlock a card of their choosing as opposed to opening boosters and hoping

DOI: 10.1201/9781003335214-5

Figure 5.1

Monetization differs from game to game, but every TCG/CCG needs a model and structure to keep going. *Marvel Snap* is trying to incentivize buying its monthly season pass as an example.

Figure 5.2 Using premium currency is a longstanding practice in mobile and F2P games and is something that all the CCGs will have as both a reward for playing and something to spend money to get. With *Hearthstone*, premium currency is used to access the arena and buy new booster packs.

Figure 5.3

The aesthetics of your card designs can also drive interest and purchasing habits. In *Marvel Snap*, not only does every card level up and gain new aesthetic details, but you can buy different art variants of every card in the game to personalize your collection.

Figure 5.4

Booster boxes have adorned many video game stores and retailers over the years and are among the primary sources of income for TCGs. *Yu-Gi-Oh!* has put out many different boxes yearly focusing on exclusive sets and rare cards.

to get it. Some games may allow you to trade cards with other players, but this is decided on a game-by-game basis.

Due to the online nature of CCGs, personalization options are also a route to go with monetization. This can include, but not limited to, special card backs, profile icons, animated characters and elements on the board, and more like with the rules and mechanics, there is no limit to how creative you can be in this regard.

5.2 Boosters and Expansions

A major aspect of TCGs and CCGs is how they are expanded with new cards beyond the original purchase or starter set. The starter set for TCGs will often come with, at minimum, one complete deck to play with and instructions on how to play. Some games may have two decks to allow someone and a friend to start immediately playing together. Sets themselves are usually fixed in terms of the cards they come with; to acquire more, you have to buy a booster (Figure 5.4).

Booster packs can be sold either individually or as part of a "booster box," which is simply buying multiple individual packs together. Booster packs are organized based on the expansion set they belong in; each set will have unique cards of all rarities. I will be talking more about the philosophy and designing sets in Section 6.5. To sweeten the deal, special booster boxes or purchases might come with an individual card, different packs, or other items. Games like *Yu-Gi-Oh!* have released not only different booster packs and boxes but also other purchases that

Figure 5.5

The act of spending money and resources in a gacha game to "pull" on a banner, like with *Genshin Impact,* have a lot of the same psychological motivators as opening up booster packs and boxes in terms of spending money to get a chance at X. The differences are with the utility that cards provide and the physical good secondhand market.

combine different booster set packs that would not normally go together and special collectors' tins with unique packs.

In terms of the individual booster packs, this is where it gets tricky from a logistics point of view. Due to the nature of buying booster packs to acquire goods at random value, there have been talks for years about TCGs and CCGs being related to gambling. The act of opening a booster pack is akin to the same concept of **loot boxes** in mobile and F2P games (Figure 5.5). To avoid legal issues, TCG manufacturers have been printing on every booster pack and booster box the distribution of cards that can appear and the probability of getting a rare card. For CCGs, just like how developers that use loot boxes and **gacha** systems must display their drop rates, CCGs must also provide that information to consumers.

Due to every game having different rules for deck sizes and rarity tiers, there is no universal standard. Here is a basic example of a hypothetical booster pack that contains 10 cards and three rarities:

- Seven common cards
- Two uncommon cards
- One card that is either common or foil rare

The average rate at which someone can pull a foil card differs based on the game. To complicate matters further, sets may introduce new rarity tiers that will be a

Figure 5.6

New expansions and, by extension, new cards are what drive the popularity and continued income of TCGs/CCGs. *Pokémon TCG* sets not only are purchasable but also factor into a rotating ban list that I will discuss later in the book.

factor in card distribution. Sometimes, card manufacturers may print a limited-run booster box and packs that can come with more cards, guaranteed higher-rarity cards, exclusive new art for cards, or all the above. Regardless, as the designer of a game, you must always show the rates for the different rarities when someone is making a purchase.

Booster sets are also important when it comes to balancing and playing the game under different **formats**, which I will discuss more in Section 9.2. For games that feature multiple formats, there may be exclusive sets and boosters that are considered legal to play. For tournament play, cards from certain sets may be banned or rotated in and out, a practice I will discuss in Section 8.7. New sets are vital to keep people interested in playing and to prevent any one card or strategy from remaining the dominant one (Figure 5.6). CCGs will allow players to purchase booster packs of their different sets using premium currency, and they are still required to tell the consumer what they should expect from opening a pack.

You may think to yourself that purposely limiting the printings of cards would lead to more money from people trying to collect the best cards, but this can backfire because of the design of the game. At the end of the day, a TCG/CCG that cannot be easily played due to players not being able to collect enough cards to build viable decks is a game that people will not be playing. From a balancing standpoint, you do not want to create cards that are both rare and unbeatable by everything else, as that would create a huge imbalance with your design, and I will talk more about this in Section 8.4.

5. How Monetization Works

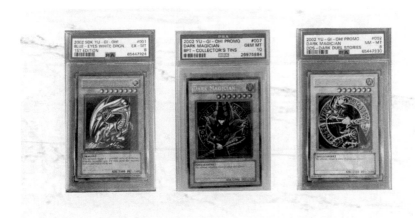

Figure 5.7

Graded cards are an essential part of any hardcore collector's collection. Getting a high grade on a card will tremendously increase the resale value.

Even though older sets may not still be allowed in normal play, that does not mean their value goes away. In fact, another area unique to TCGs comes with their secondhand markets.

5.3 The Secondhand Market

One aspect that is unique to TCGs compared to CCGs and other genres is the secondhand market for cards. The nature of TCGs is that with new expansions and sets, which I talked about in the previous section, there is an always-expanding number of new cards entering the market and old cards that are no longer used. Just because a card is not allowed in tournaments or standard play does not mean its value is gone. Besides playing with these cards in a casual setting, for every major TCG, there is a thriving and lucrative market for these cards. For fans, it often comes down to the collectible drive to own all the cards or have a collection of extremely rare cards. There are people who only collect unopened booster boxes and packs to then sell to people looking to complete their decks or collect rare cards.

Like with any physical media, the price comes down to rarity as well as condition. Since the market includes banned cards (a topic I will discuss in Section 8.7), elements like power and utility for the game presently do not matter. Much like the comic book market, cards from earlier printings, which were rare back in the day, in fantastic condition will fetch a higher price. Just like with any memorabilia, there are companies that specialize in grading cards, which increases their value but also makes them unplayable due to their being sealed in a case (Figure 5.7).

Figure 5.8

Tabletop games and TCGs require far more attention to manufacturing and distributing compared to digital titles and are why they can be harder to profit from.

This is not something that you, as a designer, can directly control, with the exception being the actual number of cards that are printed. Because reselling occurs on the secondhand market, the creator will not be seeing any of this money; the creator is only entitled to the original sale as per the **first-sale doctrine**. However, if your game becomes popular enough to cultivate a market like this, it can lead to continued sales from people buying boosters and expansions, hoping for rare cards to then turn around and sell.

5.4 The Logistics of TCGs

While TCGs can bring in a lot of money, that can be offset by the additional costs that come with handling the distribution and manufacturing of cards and sets. The details of manufacturing and printing are off topic for our design book, but it is important for any prospective TCG or tabletop game designer to understand the basic logistical hurdles.

The beauty of video games switching to a digital model has been cutting down on the production costs that goes with retail. For TCGs, as a physical good, this means you are not only spending money during development and for your employees but also to get cards manufactured and shipped all around the world (Figure 5.8).

5. How Monetization Works

Unless you are big enough and profitable enough to have your own manufacturing factory or printing department, you will need to work with a manufacturer. Manufacturers of physical goods all around the world will work with different kinds of games, have access to specific materials, and, of course, have different costs for production.

One of the harshest lessons learned by indie developers who did Kickstarters during the 2010s to produce physical goods was the challenge and cost that came with them. Every factory will have different costs of working with them, and this includes but is not limited to:

1. How many copies of the product you are printing. Factories will always offer discounts for larger orders and charge more for smaller production runs.
2. What materials you are requesting everything to be made from and whether you will use higher-quality materials for specific products
3. When you need the order done and where the finished production run will be shipped
4. Whether you will need sets done in other languages and, if so, how many of each language you will need
5. What the design of the box is, what will be in it, and how things will be organized and placed

The challenge from a production standpoint is getting enough goods manufactured for worldwide distribution but not printing so many that it eats up any revenue earned. If need be, you have the option to have additional printings done, but you will need to set up another manufacturing deal with the factory.

With that said, getting production finished does not mean you are done. The next step is to ship product to stores and directly to people if you offer the option to buy it. Factories do not handle the logistics of fulfillment; for that, you will need to either do it yourself or work with a fulfillment company that handles it for you. The largest TCGs may handle the manufacturing and fulfillment of sets within the company structure itself, but this is an option only for the largest and most profitable games.

The best advice I received from tabletop designers in this regard is to do the research early and contact multiple factories and fulfillment centers to get a good understanding of the cost and the time frame for when everything will be done. The worst thing you can do from a management standpoint is to wait until after you have taken preorders or done a Kickstarter before locking down a contract.

Tabletop-related Kickstarters are some of the highest-earning campaigns seen over the 2010s, and a lot of that cost and earnings come from the attrac-

Figure 5.9

Kingdom Death: Monster is one of the most heavily funded Kickstarter projects, raising more than $12 million over its campaign. Part of that came from the multitude of figurines and physical content promoted for the game.

tion of having quality physical goods and the knowledge that getting them created and shipped is expensive (Figure 5.9). If you are going to build a TCG or tabletop game and do not prepare for manufacturing and fulfillment, you can easily sink your game's chances of success and burn through any profit earned.

6

Designing Cards

6.1 The Basic Template

Card designs for TCGs/CCGs can differ based on the game and the style/theme the designers are going for, but there are several universal details that every kind of card must have. There is no exact order that I am going to talk about in this section, but every part must be featured somewhere on the card itself.

Let us start with the aspect that everyone will see immediately—the image (Figure 6.1). Every card that will be created for your game must have a corresponding image. The complexity of the game and the card itself will often determine how big the image will be on the card. For a resource card, like a basic land in *Magic*, the image can take up the entire card front because there are no advanced rules for basic cards. Most card-based games will dedicate, at minimum, 50% of the card to the art itself and leave the remaining half for descriptors

Figure 6.1

Disney is working on its own TCG at the time of writing this book called *Lorcana*, which I could not get access to look at. However, the cards themselves are perfect examples for reviewing the details that go into designing the front of a TCG card.

DOI: 10.1201/9781003335214-6

Figure 6.2

Card designers must make use of every available space on a card to present something that is clean to look at yet still has all the rules and mechanics for using said card.

and text. One area in which CCGs offer an advantage in terms of art is that due to the game's UI, it is possible to design cards that are 100% image and then use a secondary window to display the rest of the information. However, if you are building a TCG or tabletop game, you must leave enough room on the card to display all important information about how that card works.

After the image, the next detail is distinguishing elements via color, not to be confused with the coloring of the card art. Color is a popular way of quickly distinguishing the type of card or whether the card belongs to a specific faction. In *Gwent*, because the card art takes up the entire front, every card has a border color around it to represent the different rarities. In *Magic's* case, every card printed will use one of the five colors, or more for specific cards, to let the player know easily what faction(s) that card belongs to (Figure 6.2). In *Yu-Gi-Oh!*, because there are no factions, the colors are used to distinguish different types of cards and different categories of monsters. If a game introduces a new kind of card or even a new faction, you'll need to use new colors to distinguish them from the others.

The next point is the cost of using the card. I will talk more about what resources mean in Section 8.2, but for now, most card-based games will require the player to pay a cost to play a card each turn. There are exceptions such as *Gwent*, where instead of a cost to play a card, players' decks are limited based on provision, which I talked about in Section 4.4. *Magic* uses both numbers and symbols for costs—the numbers denote the use of any land card, and the symbols are color-specific land cards used to play a card. In *Pokémon TCG*, cost is tied to the energy mechanic of using abilities, which the game shows via symbols next to each ability.

6. Designing Cards

Figure 6.3

On each of these *Pokémon: TCG Online* cards, you can see the different costs and abilities in a way that is clean and easy to understand.

For cards and card games that have characters that can attack, defend, or both, you will also need a section of your card dedicated to stat values. Due to their importance, these numbers are often made bigger than the resources and can take up one or multiple corners, depending on the style of the game. If a card can perform different kinds of attacks, you will need to show that and the respective values on the cards (Figure 6.3).

The last element is any use of text on the card itself. The most common example is the title of the card. The font or coloring of the title can also be altered for foil or higher-rarity versions. Depending on the game itself, text can be used to identify the kind of card it is or if it belongs to a specific species in your game. While the image takes up the bulk of the card, the other major area is the text box. The text box serves two purposes: it provides all information about how the card is used and any keywords, and this is where the flavor text will go.

Starting with the information, this is the part of the card that goes into detail about any special rules/mechanics or abilities the card has access to. For more advanced cards, it is possible to fill up most of the box with all the different abilities that go into the card. I'll talk more about keywords in the next section, but they provide an easy way to identify specific mechanics or conditions in your game. Flavor text is about the lore of the card and how it fits into the story and world that your game takes place in. This can be as simple or as advanced as you want it to be, and it will take a good writer to create interesting flavor text. In terms of legal info, there is often smaller text to credit who illustrated the card, the card's place in the overall set, and copyright information related to it and to the game. Every card will

Figure 6.4

Pokémon: TCG, the physical and online version, is a good example of a TCG/CCG that uses symbology to reduce the need for text. On this card, you can see the symbol for the type of *Pokémon*, the cost to use its abilities, and even the cost for retreating and what type will deal double damage to it.

also need to have art on the back, which is often the logo of the game or something generic that appears on every card printed.

An important detail for every card design and the game's overall design is the use of symbology. To reduce the number of words needed, cards will often make use of different symbols to represent information, such as resource costs, type of card, rarity, and more. This is another aspect that differs between card games. The symbology of a card game is designed to be universal across the entire game (Figure 6.4). Just like in good UI/UX design, you want to use as few words as possible. This will make your cards cleaner and make it easier to follow what a card does.

There is one final point I want to make in this section. Whatever style of card a game makes use of for its first printing/edition does not mean that style is fixed forever. As these games evolve with new card types, new rules and mechanics, and even new factions/classes, card designs can be altered. If a style proves to be unpopular or you want to update the design to modernize it, you as the designer are not stuck with it. Do not be afraid to try new styles, themes, etc., as it is hard to predict what fans will resonate with.

It is also important to be aware that changing the style of your cards is a massive deal and something you should not take lightly as a designer. This can and will take a lot of time and money and you do not want to be doing complete redesigns of your cards with every new set. If you do want to experiment with a new style without changing your core set of cards, you can create new designs specifically for other formats of play and say that these cards are format specific.

Figure 6.5

Keywords is a concept you need to decide on during the development of the design of your game and mechanics. This is not something that you can just decide to start doing with your cards five sets in. Even all the redesigns of *Gwent* implemented keywords into all the factions and cards.

6.2 Creating Keywords

An essential aspect of designing a card game is keywords. Keywords in this respect are shorthand for unique mechanics/rules or modifiers that exist within your game that are limited to specific cards/card types. Here are a few possible examples:

- Flying—Cards with "Flying" can only be targeted by spells or other cards with "Flying" or "Anti-air"
- Fireborn—Card is immune to fire damage, but all water-type damage is doubled
- Cowardly—Card can only attack if there are no defending cards on the opposing field

This is an area of TCG/CCG design in which there is no limit to the variety of keywords you as the designer can create for your game (Figure 6.5). In terms of the application of keywords, this section is going to be on the shorter side, but I will go into detail about the approach to balance in Section 8.4.

Depending on the design philosophy of the game, keywords can be race or faction specific. In *Gwent*, a key appeal and design process of the game is that every faction has multiple ways of playing and access to keywords unique to it. A popular marketing and design strategy is to have new keywords introduced or focused on in specific expansion sets to make those sets more appealing to consumers and help control where these keywords can show up in your game.

As I talked about in Section 3.3, the interaction, or card dynamics, is where the depth and complexity can be seen in CCGs/TCGs. It is time for another example of how card interactions, this time with keywords, can lead to interesting situations:

Player A summons this monster:

- Ilzath the Undying Golem
  - Cost—7 mana
  - Rarity—epic
  - Type—creature
  - Stats—2 attack, 10 health
  - Effects—taunter: ground creatures must target this card when attacking; Regeneration: creature fully recovers health during the draw phase; Magic Ward: immune to all magic-type damage; First Strike: "First Strike" creatures do their damage first in combat

This would be an example of a card designed to provide the player with a highly effective defense that, unless the opposing player can produce 10 points of damage in a single turn, they will not be able to easily beat it. With that said, despite the keywords on this card, there are in fact many ways, depending on the design and other keywords and mechanics in the game, to completely disregard this card as a major threat. And it is that variety that makes CCGs and TCGs interesting to play and keeps their players coming back for more.

For the sake of our lesson, let us imagine some keywords that, if applied to a card, would be a hard counter to Ilzath:

- Flying—cards with "flying" ignore creature cards except for "Anti-air" and "Flying" during combat
- Last Breath—creature is immortal and wins any fight but is sent to the graveyard after opposing creature is defeated
- Poison Touch—a creature hit by "Poison Touch" is instantly defeated

And there are many more examples I could put here, even coming up with spell-type cards that would get around its magic ward keyword. If you are hoping for a standardized list of keywords that you can use for your game, there are not any. This is where the card design and variety of your game will grow. When you combine keywords with unique or general effects, it can lead to situations that can spiral out of control from a balance standpoint.

With the "Last Breath" keyword example, let us imagine that a few sets later, the game introduces a new keyword that can be applied via a spell card:

- Undying—when a card with "Undying" goes to the graveyard, return to the player's hand on the following draw phase

By putting this keyword on a card that already has Last Breath, we effectively create an infinitely appearing creature who will always win every fight it has. There is also

Figure 6.6

Every longstanding TCG/CCG will have the challenge of balancing new cards with old cards and giving new players a chance to compete with existing ones. *Magic: The Gathering Arena* and other CCG versions of TCGs will do their best to create a balanced atmosphere for everyone.

another problem—what happens when two creatures with "Last Breath" fight each other? For the former situation, I will be discussing the challenge and near-impossible task of futureproofing your card balance in Chapter 8 (Figure 6.6). For the latter problem, this is where, as the designer, you need to be very clear on how examples of the keyword can work. To fix this potential issue, we need to add one more line to the keyword text: "If defending creature has 'Last Breath,' both cards are defeated."

Besides creating new cards for future sets and expansions, this is also where new keywords will be introduced and integrated into the game. Due to their utility from a balancing standpoint, a card with any keyword on it provides more value to the player than a card that does not with the same stats and cost. This can lead to situations in which older cards that are still in circulation no longer have viability with the current state of the game, as their ability to interact with other cards is lessened. This is one factor that has led to banning cards in games, which I will come back to in Section 8.7.

6.3 The Different Kinds of Cards

Like keywords, the different kinds of cards you can create for your game have limitless potential, and that also means that for this book, there is no fixed list for what should be included in your game. Broadly speaking, we can first define cards between two categories: cards that remain on the field once they are played and those that are removed.

Figure 6.7

The different types of cards in your game are not set in stone during development. *Yu-Gi-Oh!* has expanded its card types over the years and with different expansion sets.

For any card game that features characters, these cards will remain on the board until they are removed by some means, such as losing in battle (Figure 6.7). In *Magic*'s case, land cards that also count as resources also remain fixed on the board once they are played and are only removed by specific card effects. Cards that produce a one-time effect or change something about the board itself would be cards that are moved to the graveyard and do not stay on.

However, these categories quickly break down when we look at popular TCGs/CCGs. As a quick rundown, here are just some of the many examples of advanced card types featured in games.

- Fusion Monsters: a monster in *Yu-Gi-Oh!* that requires the player to have specific cards on the board and the "Polymerization" spell card to summon and does not count as a "normal summon"
- Enchantments: a spell card in *Magic* that attaches to a creature card enhancing or changing its properties while equipped
- Weather: a type of card in *Gwent* that adds a weather condition to one or both sides of the playfield. Cards under weather effects can take different damage based on the effect itself.

It is common in TCGs/CCGs to introduce new card types alongside new sets that can greatly change the **meta** of a game. Card types can be available either for play in all formats or for specific ones depending on the design of the game. Depending on the game itself, there may be hard rules for how decks can be built

6. Designing Cards

Figure 6.8

Magic: The Gathering has used different sets as a way of exploring new themes, creating new card types, and even adding IPs from other franchises to the game.

around the different card types that I'll discuss in Section 8.1. Just like everything I have talked about, introducing a new card type is not a small task or easy to balance. Most TCGs/CCGs starting out might begin with one or two card types, depending on if they have a separate one that acts as a resource, and the overall complexity of the game. This is something that you need to figure out during the development of the rules of your game and before you start manufacturing and fully producing your game.

The challenge of introducing new card types is how they fit within the rest of your game. Part of this has to do with the overall balance, which I will talk about in Section 8.4, and the other is about when to ban cards, which I will also come back to. The reason new card types are introduced is to add new strategies and options to a game that were not there without them (Figure 6.8). If those options are inherently better than the content that is in the game or, worse, cannot be beaten with the older options, you are setting up your game to become imbalanced.

Hearthstone is a good example of this. For several years, the game allowed players to compete against each other with access to all the sets that were currently available. This created a situation in which unless the player bought the newest set, they would find themselves going up against players with far superior options and tactics. This would lead to them creating different formats of play that limited what cards were available to play and has become standardized among competitive TCG/CCGs. Using formats to limit what cards can be used or specifically having cards unique to the format will be discussed in Section 9.2.

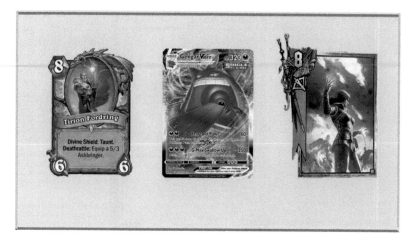

Figure 6.9

Rarity is the driving force when it comes to collecting cards, and every game under the sun has its own rules for drop rates, balancing, and what aesthetics go into a rare card.

Marvel Snap is categorizing cards into different "pools" based on the player's overall collection level in the game. Once a player has every card in a pool, they will start finding the newer pool cards as rewards for playing—with the depth and complexity of the cards growing pool by pool. While this is an alternative, it also presents a problem with not everyone in the same pool having equal access to the cards they need and their decks suffering because of it.

For the rest of this book, I am going to use the following definitions when talking about card types:

- Creature: any card that represents a character on the board that can attack or defend
- Spell: a card that either does something to the playing field or affects creatures

6.4 The Impact of Rarity

In the last chapter, I spoke about rarity from a card **aesthetics** and pricing point of view, but it is time to start talking about what rarity means from a balancing one. Just like gacha games, TCGs/CCGs will have different rarity tiers to categorize cards. Depending on the game, there can be multiple rarity tiers and various ways to differentiate one from another (Figure 6.9). Some common terminology that games have used for tiers in order of least to most rare would be: Common, Uncommon, Rare, and Legendary. Whatever you call your tiers is less important than the number of them that exist in your game.

Figure 6.10

Gwent is a good example of using rarity as a form of complexity and depth. There are very few gold cards in the game that just give the player points on the board and are instead about creating specific card combos and strategies that can backfire if you don't understand them.

There are two mindsets for how rarity will work in a card game. The first is that rarity directly equals power: the rarer the card, the more power that card has compared to similar-cost cards. This is the simplest design method and, oftentimes, the worst way to designate rare cards in a game. If there is a two-cost creature card that is very rare with stats equaled to a five-cost common creature, that can easily destroy the balance of the game between those who have it and those that don't.

For games that have multiple tiers between the lowest and the highest, this is not as sharp a blow if the second rarity tier has cards better than the first, as those cards should be far easier to acquire. The first tier of cards will typically have no keywords or very basic ones attached, and starting from the second tier is when cards start to have more interesting keywords and mechanics. For every rarity tier that is active in your game, expansions should have cards for all the current tiers.

The other mindset that leads to more interesting design but is harder to do is that rarity is tied to card complexity (Figure 6.10). Yes, the player is getting a stronger card compared to a lower-tiered one, but the rarer card features more mechanics and rules and is harder to use effectively. Rarer cards in this respect lead to advanced strategies that can win the game but could easily backfire if the player does not know how to use the card right. Here is a hypothetical card example:

- Frenea the Forest God
- Type: creature
- Rarity: Legendary
- Cost: 4 of any land cards, 5 green land cards (9 cost total)

Figure 6.11

When you design cards around having a unique power or utility, it gives them far more staying power compared to games that just keep upping the power curve. *Pokémon TCG*'s rarer cards may be stronger than normal ones, but they also come with unique abilities that must be factored into their usefulness.

- Stats: 6 attack, 6 health
- Effect: When Frenea is summoned, gains +1 attack and health for every nonland green-card active. Cast "thorn shot"—do 2 points of spell damage to any creature, repeat X times for the number of green creatures in both graveyards.

For this example, Frenea starts with weaker stats for their cost compared to other 9-cost creatures. However, the utility that they bring with just a few green-type creatures or active spells can easily snowball out of control. What you do not want to happen is your game turning into an arms race of who can play the highest-tiered cards first.

Due to the power that high-rarity cards bring, many CCGs/TCGs will limit the player's ability to field them in a deck. Oftentimes, this is done by having a hard limit per rarity tier and preventing the use of multiple copies of the highest tier, but as with the rules discussed in this chapter, there is no one "right" set of rules for your game. If you would like to introduce new rarity tiers specifically for different aesthetics and not involving gameplay, that would fit more along the lines of what was discussed in Chapter 5.

As I will discuss in Section 8.4, the challenge of rarity and adding more tiers is that as new cards and tiers are added, it can make older cards irrelevant to the game. Like gacha games discussed in *Game Design Deep Dive: F2P*, you want to be very sure that your design will remain stable if you decide to create a brand-new game-affecting rarity tier. Therefore, designing around utility as opposed to direct power leads to more interesting choices, as the unique utility of a rare card is not something that goes out of style (Figure 6.11). However, as new cards and rules

Figure 6.12

An advantage for CCGs is being able to create solo-based content for games, like *Hearthstone's* first expansion/adventure pictured here. It allows people to play something other than a standard match while earning cards at the same time, and they are not dependent on other players to enjoy it.

are created, older utility may lead to unintentional balancing issues and is often an area where cards will get banned.

6.5 Creating Expansion Sets

Throughout this chapter, I have talked about the individual card design, but any long-running TCG/CCG never releases cards one or two at a time but in an expansion. The only exception to this rule currently is *Marvel Snap* which puts out individual cards frequently as opposed to a lot at one time. Expansion sets are the card game's equivalent of an expansion pack or **DLC** for a digital game. For traditional TCGs, players can acquire a new expansion's cards via booster packs or an entire booster box, discussed in Section 5.2. For CCGs, they can be a little more creative than just having the packs. Games like *Hearthstone* and *Gwent* turned their expansions into story content in which the player can fight against specific AI battles to get cards from the set guaranteed (Figure 6.12).

Expansion sets are the lifeblood of a TCG/CCG, as they provide several valuable features to your game:

1. Expansions are where you will continue to earn revenue beyond the initial purchase, which will be required to keep your company going.
2. The new cards added can be used to create new strategies or act as a form of balance for existing ones that didn't have a counter.

Figure 6.13

The philosophy or mission statement behind your set can lead to a variety of cards and designs you wouldn't have thought of otherwise. On the top, this is a set from *Magic: The Gathering* that integrated *Street Fighter* characters to the world. On the bottom, this is from the League of Explorers expansion from *Hearthstone* that was all about exploring temples and tombs for treasure.

3. Expansions shake up the meta of your game and prevent any one strategy or deck type from being superior forever.

This is the kind of content that becomes never-ending for CCGs/TCGs to keep their games going. Once again, there is no hard rule for how many cards must be in an expansion or even having the same number of cards for each expansion. There are two categories of expansions that TCGs/CCGs will have—expansions that just expand the pool of cards and those that create new rules or strategies. In Section 6.3, where I talked about card types, some of the best-selling expansions for TCGs/CCGs will create new card types that can bring game-changing utility.

For designing a set, a common philosophy used by card designers is to try and create a theme or philosophy that the set will be built around. Is this set all about magic cards, dragons, introducing aliens? There is no limit to how far you can go in this respect (Figure 6.13). Imagine an expansion about purposely giving your opponent creatures that they can use against you, but at the same time, these creatures give you a powerful advantage while they are on the board. One of *Magic's* most popular expansions—*Ravnica: City of Guilds*—introduced the concept of cards that did not belong to just one faction or color but two—providing even more deck variety.

Figure 6.14

Yu-Gi-Oh! has had a longstanding issue with balancing the strengths of cards from one expansion to the next. La Jinn, on the left, was a card in the original release that no other card came close to in terms of power for its star level. This would lead to new cards created in the first set, Legend of Blue Eyes White Dragon, that would up the stats across the board to create more answers to it. This, in turn, would lead to older cards having a problem remaining viable compared to whatever is the newest.

Focusing on a theme provides the designer with a rough template that can be explored throughout the expansion or a way to experiment with new mechanics and keywords to see how they would fit in the game. For games that have multiple factions, you want to make sure that every person, regardless of their preferred faction, will be able to get cards from an expansion, and every rarity type presently in the game should be included. Having a theme also provides players with a rough idea of what to expect from a set and whether they want those cards. People in the competitive scene will, of course, buy every set to stay ahead of their opponents. However, for games that have been around for a long time, it can be very daunting for a new player to pick up a game and find that there are dozens of different sets, each with its own rules and themes, and have no idea where to start. This is also why many TCGs will update their starter set, oftentimes annually, to feature the current cards and strategies to give newer players somewhere to start.

New expansions to your game will set the general tone and balancing of your game. What you do not want to do is use new expansions as a way of just raising the stats of creature cards or the impact of spell cards. Raising the highest possible stats in your game with an expansion will create a new benchmark for all cards (Figure 6.14). This can also lead to older cards becoming useless if the stats for their respective cost have been changed. This is another reason card game makers will issue card bans and limit which expansions can be played at the competitive level. From a design point of view, try to hold off increasing the base stats for cards if you can, but if you do need to do it, this will come with a rebalancing of your entire game.

Using expansions as a form of balancing is another popular option. As a designer, you want every faction/deck strategy to have a chance at winning. If one faction is seeing less play or the consensus is that it is the weakest one, designing an expansion with the explicit purpose of giving that faction new options to play with can be another motivator behind an expansion. This is, again, why TCGs/CCGs are like live-service games, because there will never be a point at which a company can say that their game is perfectly balanced and there is no need for additional cards. While this development strategy can work, it is important not to design your game under the knowledge that something is not working or not that good to then "fix" it with the next expansion. This can be seen as unethical design, and if you're caught doing it, it can lead to your consumer base leaving or refusing to buy any new sets.

Lastly, in terms of the timeline for new expansions, this can depend on the game and the size of the studio, not to mention the time it takes to manufacture and ship product. *Magic* has put out new expansion sets very frequently, but it also has the additional challenge of creating sets for its different formats on top of expanding its core game's cards. Just like with any kind of live-service game, you want to figure out a schedule that works best for your company and then adhere to it.

6.6 Be Creative

What makes writing this book so challenging is that as TCGs and CCGs have grown, both have evolved in different ways, and that means there are very few hard rules or foundational elements to discuss. Many of the more popular games to be released came to be simply by doing something different compared to the other games at the time, and in turn, they became another standard for designers to look at (Figure 6.15). Even the TCGs/CCGs that did not become multibillion-dollar success stories would still try to stand out from their peers and would earn fan bases because of it.

I hope everyone will take away from this chapter the inspiration to be inventive and creative with your card designs and how your game is set up. Just like the lessons learned from the mobile and F2P industries, just copying another game's design is not how you will succeed. The goal needs to be either doing it completely better or being so different that you attract your own audience. The final design chapter of this book will talk about balancing principles of card design, which are one of the few universal aspects that can be applied to any game.

Figure 6.15

The collectability and customization of card games has spread to many other genres who have also tried to strike it big with their own designs compared to their competitors. *Minion Masters* (developed by Betadwarf and released in 2019) combines deck building, auto battlers, and tower defense into one unique game.

While you can be inspired by other popular games, do not be afraid to create your own rules or invent original keywords for your cards.

How TCGs/CCGs Influenced Game Design

7.1 Deck Builders and Roguelikes

In my book *Game Design Deep Dive: Roguelikes*, I spoke about the rise in popularity of the "deck-builder roguelike" genre. I will not be focusing on it for this book, but it could be a future Deep Dive depending on how big it gets. For now, it and TCG/CCGs share similarities in terms of design and structure that are important to discuss.

Due to the turn-based nature of both, developers have tried in the past to merge the customization and randomness of card games with the run focus of roguelikes. During the 2010s, many games attempted to combine the two. *Dream Quest* released in 2014 by Peter Whalen is cited as the first example of a deck builder roguelike (Figure 7.1). Unlike the games to come, *Dream Quest* focused more on

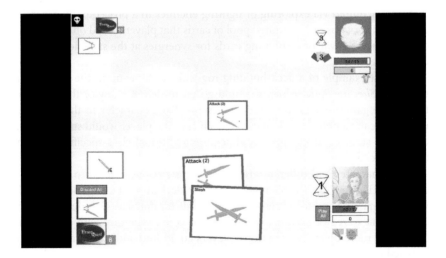

Figure 7.1

Deck-building roguelikes are some of my favorite games thanks to the replayability offered by the roguelike design and the depth of creating a deck and strategy. Even though *Dream Quest* may not be the deepest example, it is considered the first.

DOI: 10.1201/9781003335214-7

Figure 7.2

Slay the Spire created an entire blueprint of deck-building design that developers still follow. One of its biggest contributions would be changing how decks are built. The structure of building a deck during the play instead of before it would go on to be featured not just in other deck builders but in other game genres as well.

the roguelike design rather than the deck building. Battles were fought using cards that were acquired via exploring or fighting enemies in a procedurally generated dungeon. There was only a limited pool of cards that players could obtain for each class and no real way of combining cards for synergies at the same level of other deck builders.

The first example of a deck-building roguelike to blow up in the mainstream would be *Slay the Spire*, which it would go on to define many of the standards that future games would use for their designs. Each character in the game was metaphorically a unique deck of cards. Each run, the player would start with that character's standard deck and would acquire additional class-specific cards and universal "colorless" cards.

Each character had different archetypes, or strategies, related to the cards it could use (Figure 7.2). The Silent could build a deck around using the poison aliment or amassing and using zero-cost shiv cards for damage. Colorless cards had abilities that were not unique to any class and could synergize with all the characters. For more diversity of options, players could find and collect artifacts that changed rules or provided more energy for each round.

Instead of acquiring cards through booster packs and boxes, players pick a card from a randomly chosen set from shops or after combat. Not only did this provide variance over a run, but it gave the player some measure of control over what cards would be going into their deck over a given run.

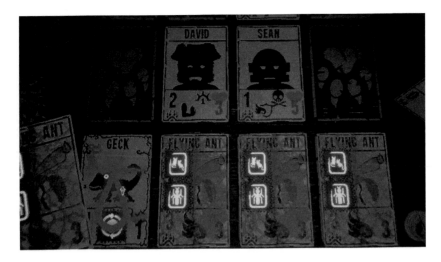

Figure 7.3

Upgrading, or modifying cards during play, is not something usually seen in TCGs/ CCGs, but it provides a powerful aspect of progression for deck builders. In this screenshot from *Inscryption*, the modifiers I have on my cards at the bottom provide me with free copies when I play them, and they gain damage for each copy on the field. This is one of many game-breaking strategies.

There are two major design differences between deck builders and TCG/CCG design. TCGs/CCGs will have explicit rules on deck sizes and card copies within a deck. In deck builders, because it is impossible to know just how many cards someone will have over a run, there are no rules for decks. Advanced play will typically focus on figuring out an exact strategy of cards and then making the deck as lean as possible to make full use of it.

Unlike TCGs/CCGs, deck builders will often allow the player to upgrade their cards over the course of a run. Some games simply have a "normal" and "upgraded" version, with the upgraded version having a cheaper cost, higher stats, or both (Figure 7.3). Some games have started to include multiple upgraded versions that the player must decide which route to go. Another option is to have a generic pool of "upgrades" that can be applied to any card, and the player needs to decide which card gets which ones. *Inscryption* by Daniel Mullens (released in 2021) lets the player apply a "sigil" to a card that confers a unique benefit, and any card can have any sigil put on it.

For a lot of the games referenced in this book, the cards themselves are there to represent the different actions or abilities that can be used in the game, but there are games that use cards also for units or characters that can appear on the board and then be commanded. Strategy games have experimented with this concept since *Age of Empires 3* (released in 2005 by Ensemble Studios) introduced the "home city" system. Every player would choose one of the factions in the game that would

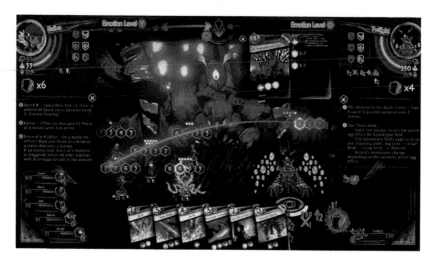

Figure 7.4

Library of Ruina may someday go into a sequel to *20 Essential Games to Study* as a game that just breaks so many conventions and rules of deck builders. No single screenshot would explain the rules or what's happening.

come with a home city that represents a deck of various abilities and units. Players would decide which cards they would bring into a multiplayer match, and these could provide bonus resources, free units, unique research options, and more.

While this section has focused on roguelike-style games, there are also plenty of deck builders that are story driven as opposed to playing runs. For these games, decks and available cards are influenced by where the player is at any given point in the game and can be altered very easily. A personal favorite of mine is the visual-novel-meets-deck building of *Library of Ruina* by Project Moon (released in 2021), in which cards are all unlocked through play and progression and which features a unique set of rules for everything (Figure 7.4).

Another variation is that instead of unlocking cards that simply exist, the player constructs a deck out of equipment that is worn by characters. Each piece of gear will give the player one or multiple cards based on it. In turn, the "deck" in these games is simply the total of cards from all the weapons and armor a character is using. Better gear could further enhance the properties of cards if there are attributes that cards are affected by. An example of this would be the game *Banners of Ruin* (released in 2021 by MonteBearo). I have even seen games that replace cards with dice, and the player collects new dice with different faces that take on the role of the deck in combat.

While deck-building-style games can be expanded with new cards and content, since they are primarily single player, there is not the same need or financial incentive to continue supporting these games with content for years as with traditional TCGs/CCGs.

Figure 7.5

Having perks, modifiers, or anything that goes into a "loadout" offers a similar sense of customization that we see out of deck builders. The *Call of Duty* franchise, among other shooters, has been using this system for years to offer players more flexibility for matches.

7.2 Customization and Perks

As I have talked about throughout this book, a major draw of TCG/CCG design is allowing the player to customize their own strategies and play style. This has led to many games adopting the customization in the form of perks or passive abilities that can change how something works in a game.

Unlike cards, perks are always limited by the number that someone can have active at one time. They can provide benefits as small as raising the player's attributes or changing the properties of how a character or weapon works in a game. Perks are typically unlocked by leveling up the player's online account.

Perks and modifiers have been used as progression for both single and multiplayer games. One of the most famous examples would be the entire *Call of Duty* franchise (developed by multiple studios) following its push into multiplayer gameplay (Figure 7.5). Players can not only customize their weapons but their killstreak bonuses and what perks they can equip, with every category getting unlocks as the player levels up. Games that focus on perks will often let the player set up loadouts that allow them to switch to their favorite combinations or build strategies before they start playing.

Multiplayer games have benefitted the most from perk systems by allowing every player to have a base set of abilities and options but letting them further tweak things to their playstyle. Games can also expand things with new perks or systems that allow for more customization, such as *Payday 2* by Overkill Software (released

Figure 7.6

While customization has become popular for multiplayer games, any kind of manipulating a character outside of its default abilities is frowned upon when it comes to competitive games. For *Injustice 2*, while it was okay to have cosmetic pieces on characters, anything that would affect the handling or playing of them was disabled for tournaments and competitive matches.

in 2013). The game originally released with just different skill trees and weapon modifiers but soon added additional perks and the option to "prestige." Prestige is a system used in multiplayer games to allow players who reach the game's maximum level to restart at level 1, but with added benefits or special personalization options to let them stand out from other players.

Prestige and perk systems can be as small or as large as the designer wants. For competitive games, this can lead to players examining every perk to find the absolute best ways to play and beat their opponents. Many **esports** tournaments and games will often disable perks and other forms of customization for competitions or ranked plays so that everyone is on equal footing (Figure 7.6).

Even the fighting-game genre has received some form of customization with the titles from NetherRealm Studios. Both *Injustice 2* (released in 2017) and *Mortal Kombat 11* (released in 2019) allowed the player to customize fighters with costume pieces and select different special moves, respectively, with these features turned off for tournament play.

The adoption of perks and customization goes with the industry's push to integrate more RPG-based systems into gameplay. These tools provide an advantage for players who need them and can pad out a game with more progression systems. For more about RPG design, you can learn about them in *Game Design Deep Dive: Role-Playing Games*.

Figure 7.7

When you have a skill-intensive game, throwing customization on top of that will lead to players figuring out what are the "best" options and basing all high-level play around them. This is what happened with *Payday 2* and the perk system.

7.3 The Limitations of Card-Based Design

The influence of TCGs/CCGs and deck builders on video games had a profound impact on the structure of games over the back half of the 2010s. However, while the implementation of card-based systems has helped to flesh out designs, they come with their own headaches and challenges.

When you apply abstracted bonuses to a reflex-driven game, it can create a bigger disparity between the different skill levels of your game. Players are notoriously good at figuring out the best ways to play a game and using all systems that the game provides to figure it out (Figure 7.7).

While using perks to create builds can help people compensate for not having enough skill to play, they can also be used to divide the player base between those that use the "right" builds and the ones that do not. It is very common in multiplayer games that have perks to create an atmosphere in which there are de facto best builds, and if you don't use those exact builds, then you are a detriment to the team.

In *Payday 2*, when the updated perk system was first released, people found that dodge-based strategies using the new perks proved to be the most effective way to play. While you could use any strategy for the lower difficulties, it was proven that for the hardest difficulty, dodge was superior to anything else. What happened was that all matches at that difficulty turned into everyone using the same build and chastising those that did not. When people are trying to figure out the best way to

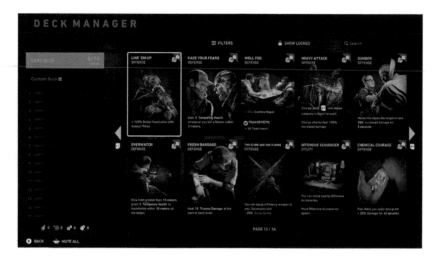

Figure 7.8

Good perk design and, by extension, card design is about each option being "good" and not having any that are just better versions of another card or simply useless. In *Back 4 Blood*, many cards provided too much of a niche bonus compared to the cards that were just all-around better.

play a game, they will look at what works at the highest difficulty, because if something cannot be used at that level, then there is no point in learning it on the lower difficulties. You do not want to create an atmosphere in which people are forced by other players and the design of the game to only play one way when there are a variety of options available.

As the designer, you are going to have to figure out not only how to create interesting perks that people will want to use but also how to balance them so that one set does not become the only one played. Because there are specific limits to the number of perks a player can use at one time, it makes it that much more important for each one to stand out so that there is no clear winner for which ones the player should take. If you have two perks: "Plus 3% walk speed" and "Increase all damage by 25%," one clearly offers more utility and functionality compared to the other. You also want to avoid designing perks that are just variations of the same thing: "Plus 5% damage, "Plus 10% damage," and "Plus 15% damage." The reason is that there is no greater choice or decision-making involved; the player is just going to pick the most impactful one (Figure 7.8).

Another issue when it comes to decision-making is if the game's design decides what the player should take and renders any other choices moot. In *Back 4 Blood* (released in 2021 by Turtle Rock Studios), the game let players create skill decks of cards for each one of the characters. On paper, this would allow someone to create different builds and strategies. However, each character was defined by unique abilities and perks—better melee options, bonus to ammo, etc. Even though there was a huge variety of cards, the "best" way was to enhance the innate bonuses of the character. What's worse was that in the release of the game, characters had access to more powerful affecting cards, but they were not available in every mode.

And lastly, as with any form of customization in games, you do not want perks to "fix" issues with your game. If a perk is so good that everyone will take it simply for the utility and ignore everything else, it may be better to just make that perk standard across characters to open the choices to your other skills. The same could also be said of a perk that provides so little utility that no one is even taking it to begin with.

Discussing balance in this regard is off topic for this deep dive, but when I talk about action games in a future book, this topic will make a return there.

8

Balancing the Present and Future of Your Game

8.1 Designing Decks

For this design chapter, I want to talk more about the balancing and design of a TCG/CCG beyond just one card. To start, it is finally time to discuss the actual "deck" of your game. As mentioned, every TCG/CCG will have explicit rules and limitations for how a deck can be built.

The word "deck" in this respect can mean two different things. The basic example is that a deck is literally the set of cards that you are going to use when playing the game. The advanced version is that a "deck" is a specific strategy that all the cards in it are there to facilitate, such as a "tempo deck," a "burst deck" etc. (Figure 8.1).

Figure 8.1

Deck strategies are a part of every TCG/CCG ever made. In the internet age, finding the best decks for any game is now as easy as finding a guide or video. With *Hearthstone*, as with any game, there are thousands of videos and tutorials for deck building available.

DOI: 10.1201/9781003335214-8

Let us start with the basic example. As the designer, you are going to need to figure out the rules for what can and cannot be in a deck. This includes:

- The minimum and/or maximum number of cards
- Limits of multiple copies of a card
- Any limitations based on rarity
- Are there faction limits?
- Are there specific cards that have their own deck rules?

The minimum number of cards does two things. It provides players with a hard number that they must take into consideration when building a deck, and it prevents someone from just creating a perfect optimized deck. A basic element of creating a deck in a CCG/TCG is the understanding of randomness. The person who can draw the cards they need for their strategy first will have a huge advantage and can oftentimes beat someone who has better cards but cannot draw the ones they need. If there is no minimum number of cards for a deck, then someone could create a 5- or 10-card deck meant to carry out the best strategy and have an almost guaranteed chance of winning. A smaller deck size for your game will inherently have less randomness and be easier to build and learn. However, this will come at the cost of depth to your systems.

In *Marvel Snap*, the game has a limit of 12 cards per deck. Creating deck strategies with such a small limit means that the possible cards that would work for it will have to be no more than 12. This limits any kind of customization options, because if you want to make use of a specific strategy, the cards for that strategy have already been determined by the design. This was a part of the design of the game to try and reduce the randomness and complexity that typically occurs in CCGs/TCGs.

On the other hand, games that feature minimum decks at 60 or more afford far more depth when it comes to creating strategies but at the cost of the barrier to entry and to learning the game. A new player starting out is not going to have anywhere near 60 cards to try and create a strategy and deck style. Making things harder is the fact that attempting to learn which 60 cards will work the best together is a lot harder than in games with smaller deck sizes. I would advise in this respect having something listed in the game's tutorial or play guide about what makes a good deck composition for your game—how many creature, spell, resource cards, etc. as a benchmark for a viable deck (Figure 8.2).

Depending on the design of the game, there may or may not be the need to institute a maximum number of card rules for your deck. Returning to randomness, the larger the deck and pool of cards that can be drawn, the less likely that someone will be able to draw the exact cards they need. It is always better to have a leaner deck designed around a specific strategy than it is to have a huge deck made up of two or three different ones. The reason is that what will most often end up happening is that the player will draw cards from each strategy but not get enough to enact one of them. Incidentally, randomness is also the reason cards that allow

Figure 8.2

To help reduce the learning curve of a CCG, they will often have different start-ing decks available when someone starts the game. These decks include all the standard, or baseline, cards for that faction/strategy and provide a guide to start tweaking as the player gets more cards.

the player to draw more cards or draw specific ones are very powerful, something I'll return to in Section 8.4. For a game like *Magic*, where the resource cards are also a part of the deck, having a maximum number of cards would make it harder to balance the need to have those cards along with the ones for a strategy.

Figuring out how big a deck should be is a part of the overall flow of a match for your game. Larger decks means more cards that can be played, and that can extend the length of a match. For most of the CCGs/TCGs talked about in this book, a single match could take 10 minutes, give or take, between players who know the game inside and out. For competitive matches in which there is more on the line, these games could take longer, with the players spending far more time figuring out each move.

Having limits on copies is something required to provide any semblance of bal-ance. If there were not any limits, someone could just make a deck of all the best cards and remove randomness from their deck. Having more copies of a card in one's deck gives the player a greater chance of drawing said card. If a deck is only made up of 30 cards, you have a 1-in-30 chance of drawing that specific card, and each copy further raises that chance. When a strategy hinges on a specific card to work, a deck may have multiple copies, but only one will be played, and the rest are there just to improve the odds.

Some games may go a step further and define restrictions based on rarity—you can have four copies of a common, two copies of a rare, and only one of each legendary. You may not need to go that far, depending on the design and cards of

Figure 8.3

Creating deck limits is a requirement if you want to have standardization for how decks will function in your game. This will impact everything from how long matches can be to what kind of strategies are even possible. Changing anything in this respect will have a huge impact on the playing of your game.

your game, but you must have something in place (Figure 8.3). Regarding rarity, what you want to look at with respect to your game is the impact that a rare card can have on the state of the match. In both *Gwent* and *Hearthstone*, the rarest cards are designed to have a huge impact on the board when they're played. If someone could just fill their deck with cards of that magnitude and play them one after another, the game becomes an arms race to just collect the best cards, and players use no further strategy. If rarer cards are harder to play and require other cards to make them work, having multiple copies, other than to raise the chance of drawing one, is not going to matter if the strategy has already been used or you do not have the other cards needed to use it.

A major design decision when you are building your TCG/CCG is going to be on the concept of factions. As I talked about in Section 6.3, there are many ways of creating card types in a game. Some games will use a faction/class system that distinguishes cards from one another—such as the different classes in *Hearthstone*, factions in *Gwent*, and the mana colors of *Magic*. Games that feature explicit abilities and/or keywords unique to a faction may limit how many factions can be in a single deck. This provides some control over deck strategies and gives the designers an easy way to differentiate the different factions. For games that go this way, there may be a separate "neutral" faction of cards that do not belong to any one faction that can be put into a deck as well. Neutral cards are oftentimes balanced around being viewed as "filler" for the rest of the deck or providing alternate utility that is not featured in the main factions. In *Gwent*, many of the better neutral cards are

8. Balancing the Present and Future of Your Game

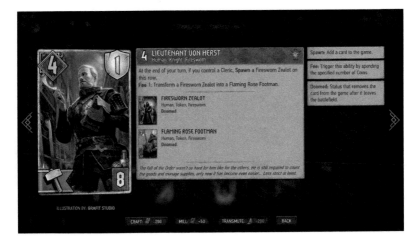

Figure 8.4

Gwent's faction system, which explicitly limits keywords and abilities to each faction, allows it to be more compartmentalized with its design. This was how the makers were able to expand the game with a new faction, The Syndicate, that uses its own unique keywords.

built as the weaker version of a faction-specific ability or keyword that can be integrated into any deck. Simpler games may just have a "hero" and a "villain" faction, and decks must choose to be either one or the other, which restricts them to those cards. The downside of this design is that it creates a hard cap on what strategies can be used in a game and reduces the number of deck types that can be created.

Whether to use factions is of huge importance for your game, and this is one area that must be set in stone during the design phase of development. This is where TCGs/CCGs do not have as much flexibility to add more to over the course of a game's life span. Creating a new faction means creating an entirely new set of cards for every rarity in your game that also must be different from everything else that came before (Figure 8.4). This also means that any new expansion is another group that must receive cards like the rest of your game. For games that feature very strict limits on cards and factions, it would be easier to create a new faction based on new keywords that aren't already featured. In *Magic's* case, due to the more free-form nature of deck building, creating a brand-new color faction that is balanced next to all the different cards, dual-color cards, and keywords in place could be considered borderline impossible. On the other hand, *Gwent*, which rigidly limits what keywords are attached to which factions, had a far easier time creating a new faction for the game.

When you're trying to decide the size of a traditional deck in your game, it will come down to how long you expect a game to play and on the average number of cards that can be played during a match. Typically, TCGs/CCGs will have a rule that if someone cannot draw any more cards because their deck is empty, they

Figure 8.5

In this screenshot from *Gwent*'s second iteration, weather decks proved to be one of the most powerful strategies around, and the game was dominated by them for a time. This was one of the aspects that was reworked for the third iteration.

will immediately lose. This prevents a game from going on forever and acts as a punishment if someone's strategy is to just keep drawing cards. There are some games in which the strategy is to cause card draw for both players and explicitly punish someone for featuring a lean deck by putting them into an overdraw position and making them lose. For simpler games that do not rely on a lot of cards being played, you can have smaller deck sizes and make each card that much more impactful. As I talked about earlier with *Marvel Snap*, games that feature small deck sizes must make each card stand out in terms of power and/or utility, or there will not be any excitement with playing so few cards per match.

Like everything discussed in this book, there is nothing stopping you from changing deck sizes and limitations over the course of your game's life span. However, keep in mind that any foundational changes to your game's rules will affect everything about your balance, and that's why you want to be careful not to do this unless there is no other option. Creating new card types with new rules to go with them can extend the depth of your game and add more flavor to decks for existing players. However, this can be an issue if you have new players going up against players with card types and options that the newer player doesn't have access to. If you do implement something that does completely change the foundation of deck building, be sure to include an option for new players in the starter decks to give them a fair chance at competing.

For the final point of this section, deck styles and strategies may be defined by the cards you create, but it will be the fans who decide which ones are the most popular. Once your game is out and hopefully being played, you can start to see where preferred strategies go (Figure 8.5). From there, it will be up to you to

8. Balancing the Present and Future of Your Game

Figure 8.6

The cost of the card should always have some relation to the impact that card has on the game. These three cards from *Hearthstone, Yu-Gi-Oh!*, and *Magic: The Gathering* respectively are all very expensive to play but make up for it with stats, abilities, or both.

decide how to expand your game with that knowledge—Do you create cards and expansions that try to add brand-new deck strategies? Or do you look to expand the cards that can be used in those strategies to offer more options and flexibility?

The popularity and power of certain deck strategies and their respective cards will come into play when it is time to balance your game, and I will return to that in Section 8.4.

8.2 Resource Systems

Throughout this book, I have used a cost attribute on the different card examples, and it's finally time to talk more about what resources and resource systems are to a TCG/CCG. As you are designing your game, you will need to decide what is the cost of playing a card. This is not to be confused with having limits on how many cards can be played each turn but whether there is a resource that the player must give up when playing a card. The implication of this system is a huge aspect when it comes to the balancing of your game, as the cost of a card has a huge impact on how easy it is to play and where it should be power-wise (Figure 8.6).

The most basic system seen in CCGs and deck-building games is having a ubiquitous resource that replenishes each turn. Some popular terms for this include "mana" or "energy," but you can name it however you like. As the match goes on, the pool of this resource will continue to grow to a maximum number defined by the designer—allowing players to make use of their higher-cost cards or just play more cards each turn. This system provides a steady progression of the match and

Figure 8.7

Games in which the resource system is built into the cards themselves will have larger deck sizes to accommodate. Often, they will create new resource cards to add further strategy to the game, such as *Magic: The Gathering* with dual land cards.

makes matches quicker thanks to the player not needing to worry about running out of resources. Games that use this system, like *Hearthstone*, typically favor what are commonly known as "tempo plays." In this case, tempo is all about maintaining a sense of pacing with the cards you play—you want to be able to always play cards on every round of a match to keep the pressure on your opponent and use as much mana as is available each turn. It does not matter if you have a game-winning strategy on turn 10 if you lose by turn 5 due to not having any cards on the field. Critics of this resource style find that it reduces strategy when it comes to managing resources and limits the different ways someone could build a deck.

The opposite concept is to build your game without any resource management whatsoever. To keep the game balanced, games that go this route will have a limit on the number of cards that can be played each turn. Once again, in *Gwent*, no matter what, each player can only play one card per turn. Not having a resource cost for your cards will mean that there is one less area that you can alter cards for balance, which is why a game must be designed from the ground up to make this system work. This is not something you can just switch a game's design to—every card must be completely rebuilt and rebalanced. Not many CCGs/TCGs have done such a thing to their game. The only example I have seen was when *Gwent* had its third redesign and completely changed the keywords and mechanics for all its cards before being released at 1.0.

In the middle, there are games that use resources as part of the strategy of play. This can be handled in different ways depending on the game, but the important detail is that the player must factor cost into the strategies that they want to use in their decks, and this can vary greatly depending on the game (Figure 8.7).

Figure 8.8

Despite the many new card rules and keywords added to it, *Faeria* never changed the basics of its resource system, and for good reason. Changing how the player acquired mana or land cards would have fundamentally changed every aspect of the game.

Once again, in *Magic*, we have the different land cards that must be put into a deck. Advanced land cards may trigger an ability or could count for one of the different colors that the player can decide when playing. In *Yu-Gi-Oh!*, cost is factored predominately when it comes to summoning higher-level monsters to the field and sacrificing other monsters to bring them out. Level 1 to 4 monsters can be summoned (unless there is a special condition on the card) without a sacrifice, levels 5 and 6 require one sacrifice, and levels 7 and higher require two, and this does not include special summoning rules. *Pokémon TCG* is like *Magic* in the sense that players must put their energy cards into their decks to draw and use. The difference is that energy is locked to the Pokémon that it is attached to and is discarded when the Pokémon is defeated.

When resources are included in the game this way, it is important to define how many resource cards can be played at once. If you do not do this, it would become possible for one player who drew two or more resource cards to play them all on the same turn and get their stronger cards out before someone who only drew one at a time. The common rule designers have used is that the player may only add one resource card to their field or to a creature each turn.

Just like with any other card type in a game, you can create your own take on resource cards and systems, such as the dual color options mentioned with *Magic* or cards that provide double energy like in *Pokémon*. Some games may introduce special resources or rules for summoning specific cards over time, but the game's basic resource system, if it has one, needs to be established during development, as it will impact the design and balancing of your game (Figure 8.8).

Figure 8.9

Hearthstone's hero powers have been a part of the game since day one and provide the player with an always-useable ability each turn. There have been times where players can alter the power, such as with this card from the Grand Tournament expansion.

In some CCGs, instead of playing cards on a traditional TCG board, players are moving units around and can control resource points on the field, as I talked about in Section 4.5. Due to the added complexity of how units interact on the field, a lot more goes into balancing and the design compared to more traditional TCGs/CCGs. Because resources are on the field, it means that a player who can get access to them sooner will have a greater advantage and chance to play higher-costing cards before their opponent. No matter how you design your resource systems, if you have them, they will become a part of how players build their decks and a factor in balance.

8.3 Designing Exclusive Powers

Part of the advantage of CCGs over TCGs that I have talked about is that they can provide more elements and options than a traditional TCG. Over the 2010s, with more CCGs being released to compete with one another and with TCGs, they have separated themselves with the use of additional effects that are not locked to any one playable card.

Several CCGs have made use of a "class ability" or "leader ability" based on the faction that the deck is using. These abilities are unique and are not affected normally by any cards on the field. Because of that, these abilities require a different approach to design and balance compared to the rest of the game. In *Hearthstone*, every hero has a power that can be activated at the cost of using mana in that turn (Figure 8.9). In *Gwent*, every faction has multiple leaders who you can assign one to be the leader of your deck, giving you access to their power during a match.

　　　　　　　　8. Balancing the Present and Future of Your Game

With *Hearthstone*, the hero powers provide you with another option to use during a turn and are meant to be used either when they are needed or when you have some spare mana left over from card use. In *Gwent*, every leader has different limits on the times you can use their powers, and they are meant to provide the means for big swings during a round.

This section is going to be the shortest of the topics in this chapter due to how specific unique powers are to TCG/CCG design. Much like factions and resource systems discussed in the previous sections, whether you want to use a system like this in your game must be decided on during the development phase. Just like adding a new faction, creating a new power like this comes with it the weight of being balanced alongside all the cards and mechanics that are already in your game. Due to the complexity, it is a rare occurrence for a game to have new leader/hero powers added after the game's released as opposed to just creating new cards.

It is possible to create cards that use their own unique rules or exclusive abilities. In *Magic*, there are creature cards called Planeswalkers that are akin to hero units in other games. The Planeswalkers have their own special spells and a resource called "loyalty" to use them. *Pokémon* features special Pokémon called V Max that have higher stats and a higher cost to use their abilities compared to normal cards. The downside is that defeating one grants the opponent more prize cards per defeat.

For games like *Gwent* that feature faction-level abilities, the typical philosophy is that each ability should correspond to one of the different styles of play of the faction to synergize with it. There are also plenty of deck-builder games that will give each playable character a unique ability they can use or start with to further differentiate themselves from one another. Adding in unique powers like this is a great way to set your game apart from other CCGs/TCGs on the market, but remember that every game-impacting mechanic you implement will need to be play tested and balanced with the rest of your game.

8.4 The Balancing Act of Card Design

If the last section is the shortest of this chapter, then this one will be one of the longer ones. Balancing the cards in your game is a task that starts out relatively simple but can quickly balloon as you introduce new cards, expansions, rules, keywords, etc.

If you have been paying attention to each of the card examples in this book, I hope you noticed how the cost and the general stats of the card are related. The first rule when it comes to card balance is that you want the cost of the card to be balanced with the stats or utility that card provides. For any game that features creature cards that can attack, defend, or both, those stats will stay close to the cost.

For example, if we have a 1-cost creature card with health and attack attributes, without any other keywords or abilities, their stats should be either 1:1, 2:1, or 1:2

Figure 8.10

Here is a collection of *Magic: The Gathering* cards arranged from low-cost cards on the top to high-cost cards on the bottom. Look at how stats differ between the two and the impact of spells and effects. You don't want a low-cost card to have a huge impact on the board state, and the reverse for high-cost cards.

(Figure 8.10). If we were to design a 1-cost creature with stats like 4:5 or 10:15, that would be a broken card, as someone would get far more value than what one resource would normally provide. The exception to this rule is if we are dealing with a game that has fixed turn amounts and small deck sizes, designed to make a match as short as possible. In these games, the stats for cards may not directly match their cost, but they should still be kept within balance of each other. For example, a 1-cost card in a short game could have stats at 3:4, and a 2-cost card could be 7:9.

For games that do not have a resource cost for playing them, you will need to rely on balancing cards based on their keywords and their stats. This can be harder, as I am about to discuss; utility is harder to judge compared to raw numbers.

The next detail is keywords. A creature card with even just one keyword on it has inherently more value than a card with the same cost and stats but no keyword. Using keywords opens the door to being more flexible with stats and can break the first rule we just discussed.

Let us come up with two examples of cards whose stats do not match the cost:

Card 1:

- Name: Coastal Turtle Dragon
- Rarity: Common
- Type: Creature
- Cost: 2
- Stats: Health 1, Attack 1

Card 2:

- Name: Angry Imp
- Rarity: Common
- Type: Creature
- Cost 1
- Stats: Health 3, Attack 3

As I have talked about in terms of balancing, with no further information or keywords, these two cards would be imbalanced for different reasons. Card 1 is a 2-cost card with stats equal to a 1-cost. And card 2's stats would put it on par with similar 3-cost cards and would be a huge advantage when played early in the game. This is where you can use keywords to give cards additional depth and provide unique strategies to use them. Let us add a few keywords to these examples and see how things change:

Card 1:

- Keyword: Water Friendly—If there are any "River" or "Ocean" creature cards on this side of the field, gain +2:+2

Card 2:

- Keyword: Blind Rage—Only attacks creature cards at random

With these keywords, the dynamic and utility of the cards have changed. Our turtle, with the right field conditions in place, can gain the stats of a three-cost card, while the imp's role now is to be an early answer to aggressive creature strategies while not allowing them to be used directly against the opposing player.

For games in which the card itself does not have a cost to summon, there are ways to use other details on the card to create a power scale. In *Pokémon TCG*, the evolution system provides an easy framework to understand and raise the power of Pokémon—the higher the evolution of a Pokémon, the higher the stats get with each stage (Figure 8.11). In *Yu-Gi-Oh!*, as I discussed in the last section, cards that are normally levels 1 through 4 do not cost anything to summon, but the levels themselves do act as a measurement for a card's power. Cards that need to be special summon (summoning using specific conditions) will be more powerful than other cards at the same level to compensate for the added difficulty of getting them out on the field.

For spell cards or any card that is an immediate effect, balancing is trickier to do. The whole point of cards like this is to provide a benefit designed to either support your strategy or shut down the opponent's. In *Yu-Gi-Oh!*, there are plenty of trap cards that are all based on the opponent doing something and the card stopping it. Due to the reactive nature of cards like this, they are often kept free or at a far lower cost compared to creature cards. Since these cards usually can only be used once per game, that is also considered with designing powerful effect cards

Figure 8.11

Pokémon TCG doesn't use cost of the card but the evolution of the cards themselves as a form of balancing. The more you invest in evolving a Pokémon, the more powerful it becomes, but this comes at the risk that you may overcommit to a single monster and strategy.

meant to be used at the right time. The exception to this point is if we are talking about a card that does something with a numerical value. If a fireball spell does 20 points of damage and only costs 1 resource to play, that would be imbalanced. However, a 2-cost spell that only blocks the next source of damage would be fair because it requires timing on the player's part to use it right. The more of an impact a spell can have on the state of the board, the higher the resource cost that should be attached to it. In games that do not have a resource cost, spell cards are designed around very specific use cases or to counter the opponent's strategy, and the timing of playing the card is more of a factor than its impact.

Speaking of timing, another factor when it comes to card balancing and strategy is the skill/cost required to do something. This is where it can get a bit complicated to describe, but the more resources that a strategy takes to work, the more impactful on the game and harder to counter it should be. One of the most common situations whenever a new card or strategy is found out in a TCG/CCG is that people will declare it "overpowered." As the designer, you want to examine the conditions and cards needed to do it and what are the counters to this strategy.

It is time for some more card examples:

Card A:

- Name—Forgotten Necromancer
- Rarity—Uncommon
- Type—Creature

- Cost—4
- Stats—Attack 2, Defense 2
- Keyword—Raise the Dead: During Drawing Phase, summon one "Zombie" to the field. Soul link—whenever a "Zombie" gets sent to the graveyard, gain +2 + 2 for the entire turn

Card B:

- Name—Zombie
- Rarity—Common
- Type—Creature
- Cost—0
- Stats—Attack 1, Defense 1
- Keyword—Undying: When sent to the graveyard, can spend 1 mana during the card play phase to put it back in the player's hand

So far, this sounds reasonable as a way of the necromancer being able to become a 4:4 unit based on being able to send the zombies to fight each turn. But let us introduce two spells to the mix:

Card C:

- Name—Poison Miasma
- Rarity—Common
- Type—Field Spell
- Cost—3 to play, 1 per turn to keep active
- Effect—While this card is on the field, all creatures take 1 point of damage when summoned

Card D:

- Name—Dark Contract
- Rarity—Uncommon
- Type—Field Spell
- Cost—1
- Effect—For the remainder of the match, all "Undying" cards can be returned to the hand for free

With these four cards in play, it is now possible to create a progressively growing necromancer who will quickly overstep the cost to stat balancing. At earliest, a player could enact this strategy on their fourth turn, playing Dark Contract, Poison Miasma, and Forgotten Necromancer in that order. If left unchecked, the Forgotten Necromancer will be able to win every fight or be used to deliver high damage to the opponent, making it easier for them to win. Further still, to stop this

Figure 8.12

This card from *Hearthstone* became the cornerstone of the Miracle Rogue strategy that dominated the first year of the game. When played on turn five originally, this gave the rogue a chance to keep playing and drawing cards and took control over the board. The nerf to the card (shown on the right) push backed the strategy by one turn to give the other player more options for how to deal with it.

strategy, the opposing player must have an answer to field spell cards or destroy the Forgotten Necromancer. However, all the cards in this example are common and uncommon, meaning that the player could have duplicates in their deck—requiring more commitment to the stopping of the strategy than to the strategy itself. And while this strategy is in effect, the player who is doing it controls the entire game, because either the opponent has an answer for it, or they will lose due to the power of the Forgotten Necromancer.

Conversely, if a strategy requires a huge investment in terms of resources and cards but can be easily countered by a far cheaper strategy or just one card, it would be too risky to try this in a competitive game. You want to avoid strategies that take one of the players out of the equation for a match (Figure 8.12). If player A can perform a strategy that player B knows is coming but cannot stop, that can lead to frustration.

As the designer, you want to avoid removing card synergies and strategies whenever possible for several reasons. Taking away a popular strategy can be seen as an act of poor balance by the consumer base, and they will not trust your ability to balance and keep the game going if they assume you are just going to remove strategies. If a card was purchased, removing its functionality will be seen as trying to steal from the consumer base after selling the card. This is the reason many designers do not like to alter characters or content in live-service games, and in the extreme situation that they are forced to, they will refund purchases of the changed content.

Returning to the Forgotten Necromancer, there are several answers to reduce its potency while still giving it the potential to snowball if it is not stopped.

1. Raise the rarity tier of the Forgotten Necromancer so that only one copy of it can be allowed in a deck at a time. If the person can shut it down once, then it is gone for the rest of the match.
2. Raise the cost of the Forgotten Necromancer by 1. This would delay the strategy by one turn and gives the opposing player access to higher-cost cards to make it easier to deal with the Forgotten Necromancer or deal with the other cards used in the combo.
3. Raise the cost of the Zombie card to 1, preventing the player from being able to play their hand and summon a zombie army each turn.

These three options would each affect the strategy in some way while still leaving the reason to play it intact. To figure out which one would work the best within the game would require playtesting.

Moving on, another aspect of balancing your game has to do with the use of card draw and card advantage. The drawing phase in a TCG/CCG is an important aspect and is part of the strategy of these games. Whoever has more cards in their hand has more options they exercise do compared to their opponent.

These games can swing very dramatically based on the cards played during a turn. Oftentimes, if a player uses up their entire hand and fails to get ahead of their opponent, they can find themselves in trouble and not have a way to fight back. Therefore, any cards that allow for the drawing of more cards are immensely powerful in a TCG/CCG. When this is tied to a creature card or a second effect on a spell card, it adds even more value to the card because the player is getting something alongside the card draw. In a lot of TCGs/CCGs, cards whose only purpose is to add card draw are some of the first ones to get banned or rebalanced. One of the very first cards banned in *Yu-Gi-Oh!* was the Pot of Greed spell card whose only power was to let you draw two additional cards when played. Even the act of card draw can be radically different depending on the game. Here is a short list of potential examples of card draw effects that a game could implement:

- Player draws X cards.
- Player draws X cards, must discard Y number of cards.
- Player searches deck for a specific card type.
- Both players can draw cards.
- Draw cards until you reach X in your hand.

Unless your game has a specific limit on hand sizes, card draw is an effect that is always good and rarely has a downside to the affected player. Card-drawing effects

Figure 8.13

Card draw as an effect in any game is incredibly powerful, which is why designers need to be careful about how much of an impact it can have. With *Pokémon TCG*, if your deck doesn't have multiple ways of drawing cards, you will be at a huge disadvantage compared to your opponent who has card draw.

allow the player to go big in one turn with the knowledge that they can just restore the size of their hand afterward (Figure 8.13). Of the TCGs/CCGs I played while doing research, *Pokémon TCG* is by far the one that has the most card-drawing effects to get specific cards out or refill your hand.

To add to this point, any card that effectively changes or impacts the basic structure of your game needs to be managed carefully. If a player can only play one creature card a turn, and you introduce a card that lets them play three, that will upset the entire structure and balance between the players who have that card and the ones who do not. This also includes cards that prevent or stop a player from doing certain phases or playing specific card types during their turn.

Another polarizing ability in TCGs/CCGs is the introduction of randomness via card effects. A foundation of TCGs/CCGs is the knowledge that a card will behave the same way every time it is played. For games that feature cards that have random outcomes, this can make it difficult to gauge the impact of cards. Let us say that you can play a spell card that has this effect:

- When played, generate and play a random spell card.

Regardless of the cost of the original card, you are playing a card to get another card with no idea of what it could be. That generated card could be several times

8. Balancing the Present and Future of Your Game

higher than the cost of playing the base one, or it could be worse than it. Introducing randomization in this respect is risky from a design standpoint. There are players who love to create chaos, just as there are those who would hate to lose due to a proverbial "Hail Mary" play that proves to be successful.

On the other side are cards that reduce uncertainty or randomness. A key aspect of TCG/CCG design is the very fact that the player does not know what cards they are going to pull each turn. Imagine a card that has this effect:

- When played, search your deck, and take any creature card and put it on top after reshuffling your deck

There are many ways for a card like this to break the balance. You could use this to put out a creature card with a keyword or effect that directly counters the opponent. If you have enough resources to summon a powerful creature, this will guarantee you get that card on the field next turn. If you have a card that lets you draw a card, you could even enact this strategy on the very same turn. This kind of effect is something that the opponent has no way to stop or counter but gives the player who uses it a huge advantage.

Another mechanic we see in TCGs/CCGs when it comes to deck searching is cards that are automatically drawn/played under specific conditions. The conditions can vary between games. A few examples are:

- On turn X, automatically draw and play this card.
- If card A is destroyed, summon card B to the board.
- When card is played, summon all other copies of it from your deck.

These cards can be immensely powerful as a means of guaranteeing certain cards to show up at a specific time or thinning your deck of cards that go together to make it more likely to draw other cards and perform other strategies.

A rare but sometimes added effect in games is creating cards that function as their own win conditions. Normally in these games, the first player to run out of life points loses, but it is possible to create cards that if their intended effect goes through, the player automatically wins. A famous example of this would be the Exodia strategy from *Yu-Gi-Oh!* (Figure 8.14). At launch, Exodia was a creature made of five individual cards. If someone had all five in their hand, they would automatically win the game. These kinds of cards are hard to balance, and if a game has cards that increase card draw or search for specific cards, they can be easier than expected to pull off. For modern TCGs/CCGs, having cards like this has fallen out of favor due to the difficulty of balancing them with the other effects in a game, especially if the game implements card-drawing effects. Another factor is if the situation to pull off the alternate win condition is so difficult or precise in terms of cards needed that it may not be worth the effort, outside of just playing for fun, to make this work.

Figure 8.14

The Exodia cards are among the most recognizable from *Yu-Gi-Oh!* because they were featured on the very first episode of the anime. While they're not as popular for competitive play, they're still popular to collect for their uniqueness.

As your game grows bigger and more complicated, you may feel the need to update cards either with a new printing or patch if it is a CCG. When it comes to changing the properties of a card, it is easier to make minor changes than to change everything on the card. Once again, working with low-number design means that there doesn't need to be a huge alteration to a card to radically change it. Simply raising or lowering the cost of a card by one value can be enough to transform how that card is played—forcing it to be played later or earlier than before, respectively. If you are designing a game that has faction systems, you cannot move a card from one faction to another, as this can upset the play of those factions.

Your goal when it comes to balancing any card-based game is to make sure that every card—and, by extension, every deck strategy—has viability in the current state of the game, but this is oftentimes a never-ending challenge. Every new card added makes the differences between the earliest sets and the latest sets more pronounced. In deck builders, even though they do not have the problem of new sets, you want to avoid having cards so bad that no one picks them or so good that they are always being used. This is also where banned cards will come in to help streamline the number of cards competitively playable at one time.

The optimal balance is that every potential strategy and the cards that go with it *can* work under the right conditions. What you do not want is for one strategy to be so easy and powerful that there is never a reason to take anything else. Just because something looks cool on paper and would radically change the state of

Figure 8.15

The weather effects in *Gwent*'s second version was considered too "safe" a strategy to use. Not only did it impact the board far more than any other strategy, the counters to it were too specific, which also limited deck building. The developers could have tried to make the other strategies as "swingy" as weather but instead chose to reduce its impact.

the game does not mean that it fits within the design, as a card like this would demonstrate:

- Name—Josh the Gamebreaker
- Rarity—Joshendary
- Type—Josh
- Cost—1
- Stats—100 attack, 100 defense
- Keywords—"Is this broken?": Cannot be targeted by any cards. "This is broken": If "Josh the Gamebreaker" is on the board at the end of the turn, immediately win the game

In this state, this would be a horrible card to introduce to a game. However, a variety of keywords could be invented to tone down a card like this. A "safe" strategy that has no risk of failing, cannot be easily stopped by the opponent, and is quite easy to pull off can be exploited (Figure 8.15). You also want to balance the use of what is known as "hard counters"—an option, enemy, etc. that completely shuts down a card type or strategy in your game.

This was a longstanding problem that *Gwent* had in its second iteration. Weather cards by the Monster deck would destroy the opposing team and completely shift the state of the board on their use. The only way to counter it was to fill your deck with weather-specific cards that did nothing else but stop the effects. This became so prevalent that the only way to correct it was to completely change how weather worked when the game was rereleased under a new iteration.

You need to be aware of the importance of certain cards based on their role in a strategy and the means of getting them. If a deck strategy is built on having one specific card or the whole thing falls apart, this can become a problem if said card is hard to find. As CCGs/TCGs go on, it is common for games to have cards that can facilitate the same strategy but at different degrees of potency. Even if the player does not get "the card" they need, there may be viable alternatives available.

The examples I have mentioned in this section can and may have been used by TCGs/CCGs in a similar fashion. If you want to keep a powerful effect in play in your game, look at ways of reducing its efficiency in some way. Cost is always a popular option, but if you change the impact of the card, that can make it less powerful as well. However, once we start talking about strategies built on the combination of cards, this becomes difficult to the point of impossible, as the card itself is not the problem; it is what the card allows the player to do with other cards. You always want to reduce the number of changes you make in your game, as every card you alter or remove reverberates out to everything else available. If a game-breaking strategy is built on four different cards, the one that affects the rest of the cards the least may be the safest one to alter or remove.

8.5 The Deck Builder Design Differences

For this section, I want to focus specifically on deck builders and the areas that are different from a balancing standpoint compared to TCGs/CCGs. Many of the same points I discussed in the previous section do apply to deck-building design. One main exception has to do with cost. Unlike TCGs/CCGs, deck builders traditionally do not increase the player's resources per turn but may allow them to get an increase as a special reward. This means cards in deck builders must be balanced around what is the starting pool of resources that the player can get access to. Many games will introduce cards that have special rules for resource consumption—such as reducing the cost based on X condition, or the card's effect is modified by the remaining resources the player has. When it comes to balancing impact to the cost, deck builders are far looser in this respect compared to TCG/CCGs—a 1-cost card could do 15 points of damage, and a 2-cost could do 26 points (Figure 8.16).

Since most cards in deck builders are spells or of the instant variety, their impacts can vary far more compared to traditional TCGs/CCGs. Balancing a deck builder is different because the player is not fighting against other human opponents but against AI enemies who will have access to their own unique set of abilities. Typically, in deck builders, there is more leeway in designing builds and strategies intended to utterly dominate the game. One reason is that because the AI has its own unique advantages and abilities, the player needs something to compensate. Returning to *Inscryption*, the game features multiple sigil combina-

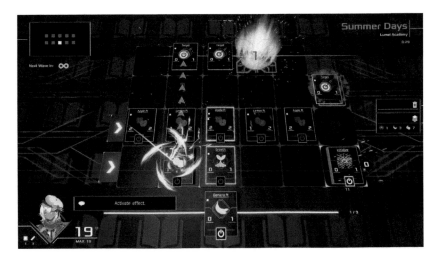

Figure 8.16

The beauty of deck builders is that they can provide the depth of CCG/TCG design and still be completely unique compared to everything else on the market. This screenshot is from *Quantum Protocol* (released in 2020 by Kaio Meris), in which every character has their own unique set of cards, complete with specific rules and keywords that the player must learn along with getting randomly chosen cards during a run.

tions that just break the game in favor of the player, but this comes with the enemy having very powerful and annoying strategies they can use. The other reason is that because the player does not have control over what cards will show up in each run, the cards must be powerful individually in case they are not able to put together a precise deck strategy.

Much like roguelikes and roguelites that I discussed in *Game Design Deep Dive: Roguelikes*, deck builders will also make use of progressive difficulty to increase the difficulty of the game each time the player wins. However, what makes this harder compared to roguelikes is that the cards the player has access to do not change. From a balancing standpoint, you need to be careful when it comes to increasing the enemy's stats, as the amount of damage the player can give or receive does not change. This can lead to strategies and cards that were useful at the base difficulty becoming useless at the higher difficulties (Figure 8.17).

You want to make sure that the cards the player has access to in a deck builder can compete against the abilities the enemy can throw at the player. If the player's defense cards can only block, at most, 9 points of damage a turn, and the very first enemy can hit for 24, using those cards would be next to worthless compared to just attacking and defeating the enemy faster. There are also more creative options for inventing cards and strategies in deck builders. In a game like *Monster Train* (developed by Shiny Shoe and released in 2020), every faction has creature and

Figure 8.17

Progressive difficulty is a popular system in roguelike and roguelite games to add more challenge to a game without overwhelming new players. In *Monster Train*, the different difficulties all lead to a far harder game to play if someone wants that challenge. However, once enemy stats start to get altered, it does restrict viable decks at the higher levels.

spell cards designed around unique strategies, and they can be combined with other factions to create new tactics and potential synergies.

Deck builders also differ from TCGs/CCGs when it comes to deck philosophy and building. Because the player is adding cards over the course of playing, as opposed to building the deck beforehand, there is more randomness to deal with. A typical strategy in a deck builder is to try and figure out what build you are aiming for in the current run and to only add cards that will facilitate it. This is where fans will focus on a leaner deck as opposed to a jack-of-all-trades approach.

Unlike traditional card games, deck builders have different rules when it comes to drawing cards. Instead of only drawing one card per turn, deck builders may take different approaches. Some games will discard the player's entire hand and give them a new one, or they could draw up to X number of cards, or something else (Figure 8.18). In a TCG/CCG, when the player runs out of cards to draw from, they typically lose the game. For many deck builders, the deck will be reshuffled and made accessible to the player again.

Be careful about designing enemies that outright counter or are immune to specific strategies/decks. There is a difference between having cards that are less effective versus outright stating that the enemy is immune to something, even more so if this option is an entire build. And if you are going to have enemies or boss fights where they explicitly punish a specific deck strategy, games today will often telegraph that to the player to let them have an idea as to what is coming.

8. Balancing the Present and Future of Your Game

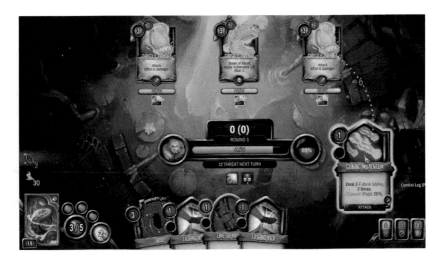

Figure 8.18

With *Vault of the Void* (fully released in 2022 by Spider Nest Games), card draw factors into your resources as well. Each turn, the player can sacrifice cards to increase their energy supply to play higher-cost cards, allowing the player to effectively play longer combos compared to other deck builders.

Deck builders are also paced differently compared to playing a match in a TCG/CCG. While an individual match may take a few minutes, the actual run could easily be an hour or longer. Another aspect of balancing games like this is figuring out what is the intended power curve a deck can grow to over the course of play. The more ways the player can deal with the enemies, the more interesting the gameplay will be. If the only way to win is to pull X card out of a pool of one hundred, it can limit the replayability of a title. One potential problem is if the enemy power curve far exceeds the player's ability to power up their cards. For example, enemies in the first five matches do, at most, 10 points of damage per turn, then they go up to do 32 points of damage per turn. Be aware of the overall power that a deck can reach and how it grows over the course of a run.

As an interesting difference, deck builders often are far more willing to give the player the ability to increase card draw via other cards or bonus items. This is because decks can grow far larger, and there are no limits of card copies in a deck builder, compared to a TCG/CCG. Instead, the act of thinning out a deck or removing cards is harder. The player may only be able to do it from events or shops, with there being a limit at each. This is meant to balance the stronger card effects that exist in these games. If someone can get a match winning strategy and remove all other cards in their deck, they can guarantee that strategy will work every time.

For story-driven deck builders, the player's ability to progress and earn new cards is going to be based on where they are in the story. Just like an RPG, you need

---

Figure 8.19

Library of Ruina is one of my favorite games simply because Project Moon plays by its own rules. This set of cards only becomes accessible if you finish the entire game to get the best ending, and even then, these cards feature unique rules and keywords not seen anywhere else in the entire game.

to balance what cards the player can access compared to what enemies can do at every point in the game. Returning to *Library of Ruina*, the game is split into different chapters, with each one rewarding the player with common and rare cards (Figure 8.19). The general progression is that each new chapter will provide the player with stronger cards compared to the previous chapter.

Just like with TCGs/CCGs, there are very few hard rules for how you should design a deck builder. With so many games that copied *Slay the Spire*'s format, it was hard for everyone else to stand out, and many never did come close to it in terms of sales. This also led to a lot of consumers becoming tired of the format and not even looking at newer examples that have fresh takes on the design.

8.6 Long-Term Support

I have spoken several times in this book about how TCG/CCG design is very similar to the mentality of a live-service game. Once your game is released and is doing well enough to turn a profit, you need to be thinking about its future. Supporting a TCG/CCG long-term will include working on new cards and sets, as well as growing the IP.

If you're a designer of a CCG/TCG, this is an aspect of your game's development that will dominate your work after release. Just like with any competitive-driven game, your game is only as relevant as the latest content for it. As I discussed in Section 6.5, your main form of long-term support will be the creation and release

Figure 8.20

While I am writing this book at the end of 2022, Wizards of the Coast has already announced and revealed its schedule for new *Magic: The Gathering* sets in 2023. This image is for the set Phyrexia: All Will Be One.

of new expansion sets for your game (Figure 8.20). Once your game is out, you should have already started to think about what your first expansion is going to be. Then you will hopefully get on a schedule that you can keep to in terms of designing and getting it manufactured.

Beyond that, if your game becomes popular, just like with live-service games, you can expand out to other properties and venues. Every major TCG/CCG has its own organization and structure when it comes to tournaments held and how players are ranked and placed. Championship tournaments are huge for consumer interest, advertisements, and sponsorships for their respective games. More than likely, you will be responsible for organizing and providing the prize money for the starting tournaments. If your game does become popular enough, and you allow it, other companies and sponsors can fund their own individual tournaments. For championships, which are worldwide, they are usually run by the developer and publisher of the game. There is also licensing your game and characters to books, TV, movies, etc., but this will require your game to already be very popular.

Due to the enormity of the work that goes into supporting TCGs/CCGs, just like live service, once you start developing content for these games, you are not going to stop. All the major TCGs/CCGs have never gotten sequels, and studios do not work on other projects to avoid splitting up the fan base or—an even worst thought—having to work on multiple TCGs/CCGs at the same time. An exception would be if you are a publisher; then it is quite common for major studios to publish multiple TCGs/CCGs that are worked on by different developers. With that said, licensing the characters and the property to other game designers is another

Figure 8.21

Warhammer might be a tabletop property, but that hasn't stopped the brand from appearing in a huge range of video games from a multitude of developers, each one exploring a distinct aspect of the lore of the property. Fans were excited to play *Warhammer 40K: Darktide* by Fatshark, a coop-based shooter released in 2023.

viable way to grow the brand. While not a TCG/CCG, the *Warhammer* franchise by Games Workshop has been licensing its property to many game studios, which each have very different takes on the IP (Figure 8.21).

8.7 Banning Cards

Throughout this book, I have spoken about banning cards, and now it is time to talk about the unique aspect of TCG/CCG design. Since their inception, TCGs have had a problem when it comes to balancing issues in games. Because cards are physical items, you cannot issue a patch if a card turns out to be too powerful (Figure 8.22). With every new set that is released, more and more cards are being put into the total pool that exists within the game. For example, as of the writing of this book, there are more than 11,000 different cards in *Yu-Gi-Oh!*

As I talked about in Section 6.2, it is impossible to predict the potential of cards for the future when the designer does not know what is going to be in the game years down the line. As keyword depth grows, you can have situations in which an innocuous card that did not see too much play when released, when combined with a newer card, becomes unstoppable.

It can become daunting for a new player to start playing a TCG/CCG and either be overwhelmed by the number of sets available or become frustrated going up against strategies that they have no available counter for just yet. Likewise, from a tournament standpoint, it can be unfair for players to compete against people

Figure 8.22

Here are three cards from the major games that have been put on their respective ban lists. The Black Lotus from *Magic: The Gathering* in its original printing is one of the most sought out and expensive cards across all TCGs. As a fun exercise, see if you can figure out why these cards were banned in the first place.

who have been playing and collecting for years and can use every card in the game against them.

To counter these issues, TCGs/CCGs will have what is known as a "ban list." This list includes all cards that are not allowed to be played in standard games or at the tournament/competitive level. It can be as small as individual cards or encompass entire expansion sets.

The ban list serves several purposes for the overall health of the game. For individual cards that are deemed too strong, the ban list takes them out of play to prevent the game from being focused on them. Banning specific sets for competitive and tournament play can alter the flow of the game at the tournament level to keep people on relatively the same level in terms of cards played. Banning older sets also ensures that weaker cards that cannot hold up against newer ones will not be played.

A ban list is not set in stone, and long-running TCGs/CCGs may revise the list from time to time. Switching what sets are banned at the tournament level also keeps the meta in flux to prevent any one strategy from staying dominant for too long. For games that are played with different formats, there can be individual ban lists per format. Some games may use a rotating ban list for their standard and tournament format which this list changes after every major tournament season. This serves double duty to keep the meta shifting and to let different sets and card combinations shine for a brief period (Figure 8.23).

Figure 8.23

There were more cards than I could show in this image, but this was the rotation that Blizzard did for the Year of the Hydra. The core set is all the cards available to everyone to make use of. When the rotation happens, the core set itself will change, impacting the cards everyone gets access to without spending materials or money. In a way, this is like the champion rotation that we see from *League of Legends*.

The decision to remove individual cards from the ban list becomes more complicated. The main reason a card is added is if its effects are deemed too powerful for the state of the game. As a TCG/CCG evolves with new cards and keywords, it is possible for a card that was once too strong to now be aligned with the current state of the game. Cards that were the lynchpin for overpowered strategies are a harder sell. If a card could facilitate an unstoppable strategy in the past, its impact could be even stronger now with the addition of newer and stronger cards. As the designer, you will need to weigh the pros and cons of reintroducing a banned card into the game, and there are cases when a card is just permanently banned. Another point is if a card is introduced with a similar effect but not as game breaking as the banned card. When that happens, there is no reason to reintroduce the older card unless massive changes are made to it.

Rotating sets in and out can only happen when your game is big enough to have a huge pool of cards such that you can ban a few sets and still have a huge variety of strategies possible. In *Magic*, there are so many sets with wildly different card effects and themes that rotating sets in and out makes sense. *Pokémon TCG* organizes rotations based on regulation marks on cards designated by letters (Figure 8.24). The Pokémon Company will issue statements for which letters are legal for tournament play. You do not want to effectively ban an entire deck type

8. Balancing the Present and Future of Your Game

Figure 8.24

Every *Pokémon TCG* card has a set symbol in the bottom left and a regulation mark (which I circled on each card). When *Pokémon* rotates sets, the marks provide an easy way for people to know if a card is valid in standard and tournament play without having to look things up via the symbol.

or strategy from your game, as that can be viewed as favoritism to certain decks, or players could accuse you of manipulating the cards played to get people to buy more specific sets.

9

The Work Outside the Game

9.1 A Development Checklist

There has been a lot of information throughout this book on various topics and logistical challenges. For this section, I want to summarize the additional work and details to keep track of separate from the design of the game itself.

By this point, you should already have the basics of your game set up: the rules and phases for playing, the design of either one full set or enough sets to build decks around. From there, you need to begin preparing the work that goes into maintaining and developing a TCG/CCG for the long term.

Unless you are a great artist, you will need to hire people who can create the card art of the quality and style you are looking for. As games grow, this can lead to hiring someone full-time and/or a team of artists. What is important when looking at a team is being able to adhere to a set style (Figure 9.1). Unless you want to use a unique style

Figure 9.1

Here are three *Magic: The Gathering* cards, from different sets and different artists. Despite that, they still match the consistency and tone of the game. Being able to find artists like this is very useful for games that are very demanding on art production.

DOI: 10.1201/9781003335214-9

for a specific expansion, you want to make sure that the art on your cards is consistent across the board. This means it can take time to find the right artist(s).

As I spoke about in Section 5.4, you will need to set up manufacturing and fulfillment for your game if you are building a TCG. Again, you want to research multiple manufacturing facilities to figure out which one will best suit your needs and the quality of the goods you are looking for. Make sure you have someone set up for fulfillment and distribution of your game to wherever you are selling it. Different territories will have different rules on importing and tariffs to keep in mind. With physical goods, do not forget that you can create different products including playmats, card sleeves, unique tins, store-exclusive boosters and more. This is an area that is specifically for the TCGs that become huge, but it is just one part of how they bring in so much revenue.

With the live-service mentality that I discussed, you should have a plan for what future sets you want to develop and an estimate of how long that will take. The biggest games become their own assembly line of set design and creation, card manufacturing and distribution, before starting the cycle again. For CCGs, while you do not need to worry about the physical production, you still need to be coming up with new sets, getting the art done, and making sure that there are not any bugs or issues with your software for how the cards will behave.

As part of the design process, there should be a lot of playtesting done with new card types and designs for future sets. Remember that you can change something as many times as you want during the preproduction and development stages of your game, but once you are selling a new card or new pack, unless there is an extreme circumstance, those cards are now set in stone.

9.2 What Are Formats?

Another aspect of controlling what cards can be used and where is with the concept of formats. A format is a specific style or way of playing a TCG/CCG that depends on what cards are allowed to be used (Figure 9.2). For TCGs/CCGs, once they are big enough to have multiple expansions and possibly a banned and rotating card list, they will have, at minimum, four formats:

- Standard/ranked play—Playing the game against other players while adhering to a banned list
- "Free play"—Playing the game with any cards, regardless of their ban status
- Tournament play—Playing the game at tournaments, which will restrict what cards and sets are allowed, but you create your own deck
- Sealed-deck tournament—A player constructs a deck while at the tournament, which they will use in matches, from sealed booster packs

With that said, many TCGs/CCGs can grow with unique formats based on ideas from fans or developed by the design team. In *Magic*, one of the formats, called

Figure 9.2

Formally supporting new formats for your game is a lot of work, but it does provide more ways for people to experience your game or an easier way to learn it if the format is designed to be that way.

Commander, restructures deck limits and play around the format. If a specialty format grows popular enough, the game can release specific expansions and boosters that are meant for that format, but sometimes, cards can be used across formats depending on the rules of the game. Another option is to create a format specifically for newer players or for faster matches. *Yu-Gi-Oh!* had a format called "speed duels" to provide an easier entry point for newcomers, with most of the cards also playable in the normal format.

Depending on the format, there may be additional or different rules for deck sizes and limits. A popular option for tournament play is having a "side deck," which is a small pool of additional cards that players can swap in and out of their main deck between rounds in a match. Some games let the player simply build multiple tournament decks, and they must switch from deck to deck each round during a match.

Like everything I have spoken about in this book, once you get past the initial rules and function of formats, it is possible to create a wide variety of plays. Many CCGs will offer scenario modes for the player to fight against the AI with specific conditions (Figure 9.3). This includes the special battles and expansion content I discussed earlier with *Hearthstone* and *Gwent*. A popular universal mode seen in plenty of games is called "puzzle," where the player is given a set board with a fixed hand and is asked to figure out how to win within X number of turns. This provides a fun diversion and, at the same time, teaches a player about advanced rules and combinations.

Figure 9.3

Puzzle modes and other single-player-based content provide an alternative to ranked matches and multiplayer matches and can provide the player with additional rewards. *Faeria* had the most in terms of puzzle content and even expanded it with DLC.

Lastly, you can use formats to introduce advanced ways of playing your game. While many TCGs/CCGs are designed around standard play of 1v1, some games will have formats in which you can play 2v2 or groups fighting against each other. For games with a hardcore following, there is also the possibility that fans may create formats of their own to play. If fans invent a format that becomes popular, it may pay to look at it and see if you can make it an official format in your game. However, any formats that you officially add to your game will need to be supported with custom booster sets and packs, and you'll have to update their rules accordingly with the rest of the game. And to reiterate, if a format has unique cards associated to it, you will need to define whether those cards can be used in other formats. If you do not want to support a custom format, nothing is stopping you as the designer from not continuing development of it, but this could hurt your popularity among fans who played the game specifically for a certain official format.

The four base formats are considered the most popular and standard among TCG/CCG fans for games today. You can get away with not having a sealed-deck mode, but the other three must be in your game at launch or shortly after. There is nothing stopping you from altering them to fit your game if it does play differently than other games, but these four provide both much-needed variety and ways for competitive and noncompetitive players to enjoy your game. Some games may not launch with tournament rules and a corresponding mode while they are still trying to figure out how they want to organize tournaments. If you decide to launch

Figure 9.4

Filters and easy-to-use deck managers are an important quality-of-life feature that I will discuss more in Section 9.4. When you have multiple ways of playing your game, you need to make it as easy as possible to create decks for all your different formats.

your game without them, you have a limited window before people will start to point out that there are not a lot of ways of playing your game.

One final consideration for CCGs: If you update your online client to allow people to play and create decks in different formats, make sure to update filters and your deck editor/creator to make it easier to sort cards based on what is legal in each format (Figure 9.4).

9.3 Battling the Meta

Next to competitive games, TCGs/CCGs have a never-ending challenge of keeping the game's meta going. The meta, or metagame, involves focusing on the major trends and popular strategies of a title. The meta for players is about figuring out the best and worst ways to play a game currently.

For games like TCGs/CCGs, the use of low-number design makes them very popular to analyze and makes it easy to break down popular cards to figure out the best decks, strategies, etc. For the developer, having a fixed or solidified meta is one of the worst things for a competitive game. If everyone knows what the best deck is, then everyone is going to play said deck (Figure 9.5). What usually happens when a meta becomes solved is that matches will turn into games between everyone who uses the meta deck and those that specifically use the counter to the meta. A popular term used in this situation is called a "net deck," and it is when a very powerful deck is posted for everyone to see and use themselves. Sometimes, there is the pos-

Figure 9.5

There will never be any TCG/CCG that players aren't trying to figure out the best ways to win. Even though *Marvel Snap* is the "youngest" game covered in this book, there are already daily videos and guides to making the "best" deck.

Figure 9.6

Returning to *Gwent*, the decision-making behind the third iteration is based on several factors. One was making the game easier to play on mobile platforms and improving the aesthetics of the board. From a design standpoint, the developers rebalanced all the major deck strategies to try and rein in the powerful ones and provide options for the weaker ones. This also meant making the very rare move of a complete reworking of every card in the game up until that point.

sibility of someone figuring out an even stronger counter and completely upending the state of the game, but this depends on the design and player base.

Everything that we have talked about in this book on designing new sets and banning cards is there to specifically counter having the meta of a game solved. This is the reason TCG/CCG designers will release new sets or rotate the current banned list to keep people guessing as to the best strategy for competitive matches. Even though anything goes for a free or open mode, gamers are more concerned about what is popular where it counts for their global and seasonal rankings.

No matter how "metaproof" you think your design is, never underestimate the ability of fans to break down your game. This is another reason sets must be designed around new content and keywords and not just rehash what's in the game. The longer it takes for players to start figuring out "the best," the better it will be for the competitive side of your game.

From a design standpoint, you should be examining what are the most popular decks being run in your game. If one deck is dominating everything, then you want to look at ways of bolstering the other strategies. As I talked about in Section 8.4, when it comes to card balancing, it is always preferable to make cards better instead of to weaken a popular strategy. Once again, your goal from a balancing standpoint is that every strategy should be fantastic at a given situation. What you do not want is for one strategy to be considered the best or the worst (Figure 9.6).

Figure 9.7

Hearthstone deserves a lot of credit for the quality-of-life and approachability aspects it brought to CCGs at launch. Some examples would be making the board state easy to follow, and dynamic tooltips to explain keywords. If you want any game to succeed in the mainstream market today, you must look at how approachable it is to play.

For any live-service game built on competitive play, another detail to playing these games is the difference between playing the game at the start and what it is like at later stages, when everyone has access to everything. For TCGs/CCGs, knowing that your opponent has access to every card you do requires a different strategy for deck building compared to playing against random people with unknown collections of cards. This is where the discussion on meta changes, as the people who are playing competitively will often dictate the state of the meta based on what decks they build. Following a major tournament, the meta can easily shift to the decks played by the top players.

Returning to previous points about having different formats, having modes for different skill levels can help with the overall health of your game. A nonranked or noncompetitive mode gives players a way of playing without having to worry about the meta of the game. This is the reason for competitive games to also have a "friendly match" option so that people can play with their friends or try out unusual strategies and not have to worry about it affecting their ranking.

9.4 Quality-of-Life Updates

To end this chapter, I want to talk briefly about quality-of-life or **QOL** updates to TCGs and CCGs. This is often a concept that comes up when we talk about video games, and it represents the ways to make a game more approachable. Another aspect of the live-service model is updating the game to make it easier to understand and play (Figure 9.7).

This can include updating the design of your cards to make them more readable, improving the layout of your playmats, rewriting your player guide, and so on. For CCGs, there is a wealth of QOL improvements you can make to a game or have at the start of its launch. Two important features players will use are filters and easy searching when it comes to deck building. Being able to immediately see all 2-cost cards or cards of a specific faction or keyword makes it easier to build a deck. Some games may even have the option to autobuild a deck based on certain conditions to make it easier for inexperienced players to jump in and start learning. Given the importance of deck building, the UI and system for it in CCGs should be easy to use. In some cases, the entire client itself may receive an overhaul when new features, modes, and online content are added. (As a quick aside, *Pokémon TCG* is planning on getting a client update for the online version in 2023, and the screenshots shown for it throughout this book may not represent the current version of it.)

As I discussed in Section 4.1 with the differences between CCGs and TCGs, a CCG affords you a lot more flexibility when designing the UI of your game to make it easier to understand. Games today will feature expandable tooltips so that you can see the details of a keyword, accurate battle predictions, and dynamic UIs so that you know the results of fighting and much more. While these details do not sound as important compared to building and balancing your game, good QOL features and UI design will keep players interested in playing your game. If your game is hard to understand or it's frustrating to do basic things, that alone is enough to get someone to quit your game no matter how great the actual mechanics may be. And just like with live-service and mobile games I discussed in *Game Design Deep Dive: F2P*, good onboarding and tutorials can often mean the difference between someone figuring out your game or leaving and never coming back.

A unique point about CCGs is being able to offer players free packs as rewards and milestones for playing. Because there is no secondhand market for cards in these games, it is important to provide players with access to free packs (Figure 9.8). The reasons are that it provides an incentive for continued playing, and it is often the main way new players can have a chance at building a deck that is halfway viable against people who have been playing longer. If your game features premium currency or a currency specifically for buying booster packs, there should be a way for free players to earn this. Having daily challenges has become a popular option for many CCGs.

Many CCGs will also have season play built into the online client. Seasons provide the player with a set period to play games and rise in rank. For hitting certain ranking tiers, they may receive rewards in the form of booster packs and/or currency. The ranking also provides an effective way to track people for matchmaking and to try and keep players of even skill level playing against each other. At the end of the season, there may be one final reward based on the highest rank earned, and then rankings are reset. The top players may start at a higher ranking compared to other players because of the skill they showed in the previous season. For games

Figure 9.8

Daily and weekly quests are a common design we see in many F2P and mobile games as a way of conditioning people to play daily and provide a structure to daily play. In *Hearthstone,* the variety of quests can be used by paying and non-paying players alike to get free resources

with a professional competitive scene, especially in **esports**, how someone ranks each season is also how major teams and sponsors look for players to sign deals with.

When it comes to UI design, the two most important things you should do are to (1) get people to playtest your game and see how they respond and (2) examine popular examples to see how they play and whether there are any areas you could improve.

The TCG/CCG Market

10.1 The Pros and Cons of Making a TCG/CCG

Before I wrap up a Deep Dive, I always want to speculate on the market itself surrounding the genre. In this book, I have compared TCG/CCGs to live-service games, and many of the aspects that make that market so lucrative/risky can be applied here.

For more than 20 years, we have seen firsthand just how big TCGs can get, and in the 2010s, CCGs were released that could play differently and do it at a far cheaper cost to make. For physical media today, Kickstarter and crowdfunding have proven to be huge for tabletop games and TCGs and are arguably the reason there has been a huge influx of these games onto the market in the 2010s (Figure 10.1).

In a way, this makes TCG/CCGs a little bit safer, in some respects, than live service, as you can create a prototype and pitch it to fans to generate interest and support. With mobile and live service, you are very much on a timer for people to find the game and purchase things so you can earn a profit before the money runs

Figure 10.1

Crowdfunding has done much to help the tabletop industry and continues to bring in record-breaking pledges. The Kickstarter for the game *Frosthaven* earned $12,969,608 and is now considered the highest-pledged tabletop game on Kickstarter.

DOI: 10.1201/9781003335214-10

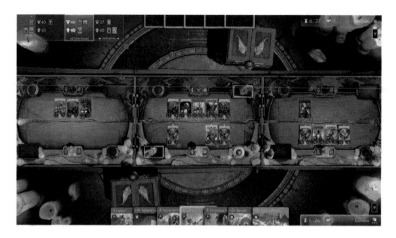

Figure 10.2

Artifact could have been a fantastic CCG, and its design was unique compared to anything else on the market. But trying to charge retail price in a genre known for being F2P was one of many nails in the coffin. If your live-service game is not immediately grabbing players and growing, that is a sign of trouble.

out. There is far less production cost to maintaining and growing a CCG compared to a TCG. You will still need to design your card layouts and get art done. However, digital cards do not need factories to produce them, and you don't need to worry about fulfillment. It is also possible that a CCG can become so popular that it could be turned in to a physical game.

However, just like live service, TCGs/CCGs live or die based on the reception they receive at launch. No one wants to invest in learning and playing a game that is not being supported or for which there is no player base. You will need to make sure that there is a stable community of players available on day one and that there is word of mouth about your game. For CCGs, having AI players or "bots" may help, but you must still cultivate a fan base. From a marketing point of view, you should be doing your best to grow your community months before the actual release, and for CCGs, make sure your client has no issues on the first day.

With so many games released these days, your game must have enough cards to support different strategies from day one while also having plans for future sets. This is not a genre that you can just walk into and expect your game to do well. Even deck builders—which are not TCGs/CCGs from a design point of view—have become oversaturated. Returning to *Artifact*, having so many complaints right at launch over its monetization and design led to players not playing or wanting to check it out, which rarely leads to games recovering with additional patches and content. This is not a genre in which we have seen games bounce back after requiring a massive redesign (Figure 10.2). The only exception was *Gwent*, and even with the redesigns that went into the game, it was still popular to play with each iteration, and even with that said, support for it is planned to end in 2024.

Figure 10.3

The back half of the 2010s was a learning period for live-service games and what I dubbed the third generation of mobile in *Game Design Deep Dive: F2P*. Just trying to repeat what everyone else is doing stopped working. Instead, games like *Genshin Impact*, among others, blew up by offering something different compared to their peers in the space.

Competitive-level players will only stick around if the game they are playing is interesting enough and has a community that will keep it relevant for tournaments and growth. If people are not playing your game to begin with, trying to entice them with tournaments and prize pools is not going to work.

For having new content added, your first set of new cards will be the benchmark that fans will judge the future of your game on. If it is received poorly, players may think that your game does not have a viable future and will leave. Just like with live-service games, you need to always be communicating to players what is next for your game and what you are currently working on.

The reward of having a successful TCG/CCG is certainly there—with the games that succeed not only becoming famous but oftentimes going on to have tournaments and more opportunities to expand their player bases and recognition. But getting that initial project off the ground and competing with the major names out there will take a lot of work and, sometimes, luck. Even with that, just because a game launches successfully does not mean that it will last long. Supporting these games with tournaments, more sets, new and updated content, and printing and fulfillment for TCGs takes a lot of money and effort. Unfortunately, even if you have a solid game, it can still take time for your game to become well-known and achieve mainstream success.

One final warning: TCGs/CCGs are like other live-service games in one aspect—games are always directly competing for a fan base. Most consumers are not going to be playing and spending money in multiple games at the same time. As I talked about in my *Free to Play* book, your average consumer is not going to leave a game they are playing just because you promote your game as "better" (Figure 10.3). With *The Elder Scrolls: Legends*, the developers were trying to beat

Figure 10.4

The game industry saw a huge bump during the peaks of the COVID-19 pandemic. Low-stakes games and those designed around easy-to-play multiplayer arrangements blew up. *Animal Crossing: New Horizons* (released in 2020 by Nintendo) provided people with something to take their attention away from not being able to socialize in person.

Hearthstone and instead ended up with a game that did not have a strong enough identity to stand out. Even though *Shadowverse* also emulated the general feel of *Hearthstone*, it stood out with its own approach and ruleset for its gameplay. There is no shame in making a TCG/CCG that does not pull in the same numbers as the major names. If you are able to earn enough money and fans to keep the lights on, then you are a success.

10.2 The Impact of the Digital Market

There is one trend for TCGs that is important for everyone to know about: having a digital way to play them. In *Game Design Deep Dive: F2P*, I talked about how COVID-19 impacted the mobile and live-service markets in a positive way thanks to more people being stuck inside and not socializing (Figure 10.4). For the other side of the coin, this impacted tabletop and TCGs because people were not traveling to conventions or going to stores to purchase and play. There have been stories of card and tabletop shops having to close due to the lack of profit.

For TCG designers, it is important for the health of your game to consider having a digital way to play your title. For the major names that I have discussed, each one has an online client version for playing the game. *Pokémon TCG* goes a step further and allows you to import booster packs you buy in the store into the online version. With *Magic*, certain sets and boosters are compatible with their current online version. For *Yu-Gi-Oh!*, all the digital cards are locked to their respective online games. While you are giving up the physicality and collectability of having the cards in front of the player, this expands the reach of your game to people who would not have had access to the game otherwise. As a personal anecdote, when I was growing up, there were no tabletop or card stores near me, which made it impossible to play TCGs with other people.

The beauty of these clients is that it makes your game not only playable for the PC but also mobile. The pick-up-and-play nature of TCGs and CCGs have done very well on the mobile market, with CCGs released on PC eventually having mobile ports made and vice versa. However, you still need to make sure that the UI and functionality work across every version of your game.

For PC games, another route is to look at something along the lines of *Tabletop Simulator* (released in 2015 by Berserk Games), a game designed specifically to simulate playing tabletop games on a computer that has also made tabletop games more accessible to people. Besides using this as a testing platform for your game, there are developers who have released TCGs and tabletop games on it as an alternate way of playing them. The game industry has seen this trend of releasing games onto as many platforms as possible, and I do feel that the days of platform-exclusive games are slowly coming to an end. For TCGs/CCGs, multiplatform support also greatly expands the consumer base and makes it easier for multiplayer games to work. Given both the simpler UIs and the importance of having people available to play, cross-platform support for CCGs should become the standard.

Conclusion

This was an interesting book for me to write and gave me a chance to check out games that I did not have the chance to play growing up (Figure 11.1). In a way, I went backward, looking at deck-building design first, having played more deck builders in the 2010s than most people even know about.

Looking particularly at *Pokémon TCG* and *Magic: The Gathering*, it is impressive to see just how long-lasting these games are and the communities and support around them. With this book and my F2P one, we can see how children and gamers today are growing up with massive games at the tips of their fingers—where games like the ones mentioned in both books are no longer considered experimental or weird projects but institutions that are here to stay as much as when we talk about companies like Nintendo, Sony, and Microsoft.

Figure 11.1

While I didn't get a chance to play *Magic: The Gathering* growing up, that didn't stop me from designing the greatest card ever for it, which I pass on to you.

DOI: 10.1201/9781003335214-11

Even if you do not have an interest in designing these games, the lessons about balance and design can be used in a variety of ways. More designers are coming around to low-number philosophy, and every year seems to give us a new inventive twist on this design. Some of my favorite and most critically acclaimed strategy games have been influenced by tabletop design and low-number philosophy in some way. It is interesting to think about how much tabletop gameplay has influenced design and the state of the industry and how we have come to the 2010s and beyond with more designers embracing low-number philosophy in many different genres.

I hope you enjoyed reading this book, and if you are interested in studying many of the CCGs mentioned, the major names are completely free to start and will provide you with hours of card collecting and deck building to learn from.

Glossary

CCG Short for "collectible card game." A trading card game that is played on a digital platform instead of in a physical space

Client For online games, the client is the software a player uses to access and play the game.

Deck builder A game that uses cards as a form of gameplay or abstracting the player's options

DLC Stands for "downloadable content." Any kind of content that must be purchased separate from the game's original pricing and can include anything that adds to the gameplay

Esports A catchall term for organizing and competing in video games at the professional level

First-sale doctrine A legal concept that inhibits an IP holder from controlling resales of a copy of their product

Format For TCGs/CCGs, a different way of playing a game using the same or different cards but with modified rules

Gacha Short for "gachapon," which is a machine in which people spend money for a chance at random prizes. It is also a type of mobile game that focuses on collecting characters as the primary monetization model.

Graveyard In a TCG/CCG, it is where creature cards that are defeated and any other types of cards, after being used, are discarded for the rest of the match.

IP Short for "intellectual property" and represents the copyright over creative or intangible assets. For video games, this can represent the franchises and characters owned by a company.

Keyword	A word on a card that represents a certain ability, rule, or mechanic exclusive to that keyword
Live service	A game that is developed with additional content and support for months and years after its release
Loot boxes	A purchase for which the consumer spends money without knowing exactly what they are getting and is heavily used in mobile and free to play games
Manga	A Japanese comic book or graphic novel
Mechanic	The "verbs" or actions in a video game
MOBA	Short for "multiplayer online battle arena," a type of game in which players compete on a team, with each one controlling one character against another team
Monetization	For video games, the additional purchases and systems tied to earning money beyond a retail purchase
Premium currency	Used in live-service and free-to-play games as a resource that is normally only earned by spending real money and given in small amounts for playing
Progression	A progression system or curve charts how someone moves through a game, growing in power and moving the story along
QOL	Short for "quality of life" and represents features that make a game easier to play that are not adding or changing the gameplay itself
RPG	Stands for "role-playing game" and is a genre and gameplay system built on in-game abstracted attributes being a greater factor for success than the player's reflexes
System	A set of mechanics all related to a specific aspect of gameplay
TCG	Stands for "trading card game" and represents games played using cards that can be bought in packs at stores or sold and traded among the player base
UI	Short for "user interface" and represents all the elements that someone will be using or looking at when it comes to playing and learning a game. Video games also make use of a "GUI" or graphical user interface for on-screen elements

Index

Note: Page numbers in *italics* indicate a figure on the corresponding page.

K

keywords, 22, 30, 36, 40, 138
  balancing, 97–101, 105, 107
  banned cards, 114, 116
  card design and, 61, 63–65
  creating, 63–65, *63*
  expansions and new keywords, 43,
      73, 91
  factions/classes and, 90–91, *91*
  rarity and, 69
Kickstarter, 13, 42–43, 57, *58*, 129, *129*
Kingdom Death: Monster, 58
Konami, 9–10, *see also Yu-Gi-Oh!*

L

League of Legends, 45
Lee, Keith, 42
Legends of Runeterra, 45, *46*
Library of Ruina, 80, *80*, *112*, 112
live-service games, 49, 74, 102–103,
      112–113, 120, 126–132, 138
loot boxes, 53, 138
Lorcana, 59
low-number design, 2, 18–20, *19*, 106, 123,
      136

M

Magic: The Gathering, 5–7, *5–7*
  banned cards, *115*
  card design, 59–60, *60*, *119*
  card interactions, *21*
  card rotations, 116
  card types and, 66
  color factions in, *6*, 90, 91
  color resource system of, 6, *6*, 16, *16*,
      23, 28, 66, 72, 89, 90, 91, *94*, 95
  Commander format, 120–121
  compared to other TCGs, 8, 10, 95
    cost to play a card, *93*, 98
  expansions with other franchises, 24,
      67, 72
  expansions, *30*, *67*, 72, 74, *113*, 116, *119*
  "instant" cards, 17
  mechanics in, 23
  monetization, 8, 49
  online, 7, *7*, 65, 132–133
  rules in, 15, 89

special cards in, 97
starter packs and premade decks, *28*
strategy in, 28
in various formats, 34, *121*
manga, 9–10, 49, 138
manufacturing and distribution, *18*,
      56–58, 67, 120
Marvel Snap, *27*, *47*, 48, *50*, *51*, 68, 71, 88,
      92, *124*
Massively Multiplayer Online Games
      (MMOGs), 12, 42
mechanics, 23, 24, 29, 138, *see also* card-
      based game design; keywords;
      systems
Media Factory, 8
Mega Crit Games, 20
Meris, Kaio, *109*
meta of a game, 66–67, 72, 115, 123–126
Minion Masters, 75
mobile games, 36, 37, 49, *51*, 53, 74, 127,
      128, 129, *131*, 132–133
monetization, 39–40, 49–58, 138
  boosters and expansions, 52–55
  downloadable content (DLC), 71, *122*,
      137
  first-sale doctrine, 56, 137
  free-to-play (F2P) games, *51*, 53, 74,
      128
  gacha games, *53*, 53, 68, 70, 137
  logistics of TCGs and, 56–58
  micro- (and multiple) transactions,
      49–52
  premium currency, 36, 39, 49, *51*, 54,
      127, 138
  the secondhand market, 55–56
  seasonal play and season passes, 49, *50*,
      127–128
Monster Train, 109–110, *110*
MonteBearo, 80
Mortal Kombat 11, 82
Mullens, Daniel, 79
multiplayer games, 26, 80, 81–82, 83, 133
  Massively Multiplayer Online Games
      (MMOGs), 12, 42
  multiplayer online battle arenas
      (MOBAs), 44–45, *46*, 138

deck-building roguelikes, 44, 77–80, *77*, *78*, 109, *110*
role-playing games (RPGs), 19, 82, 111–112, 138

S

Sapkowski, Andrzej, 40
sealed-deck tournaments, 120, 122
seasonal play and season passes, 49, *50*, 127–128
Second Dinner Studios, 48
self-published games, 13
Shadowverse, 37–39, *38*
Shiny Shoe, 109–110
"side decks," 121
single player, 43, *71*, 80, 81, *122*
Slay the Spire, 20, 78, *78*, 112
Solomon, Jake, *20*
Sparkypants Studio, 44
"speed duels," *121*, 121
Spider Nest Games, *111*
starter sets, *28*, 29, 52, 73, *89*, 92
Steam, 42–44
strategy games, 42–43, 79–80, 136
Street Fighter, 72
systems, 138, *see also* customization/ personalization; resource systems
    card evolution systems, 8–9, 37, *38*, 99, *100*
    card upgrading systems, 20, 38, 79, *79*
    factions/classes, 23, 35, 37, 78, 90, 91, 96, 106
    "level up" systems, 45, *46*, *51*
    perk systems, 2, 81–85
    "prestige" system, 82
    weather system in *Gwent*, 66, *92*, 107–108, *107*

T

tabletop games, 1–3, 5, 13
    cards in, *34*, 34, 60
    crowdfunding of, 129, *129*
    impact of the digital market on, 132–133
    influence of, 136
    IPs, *114*
    low-number philosophy in., 18–20, *19*

manufacturing and distribution of, 56–58, *56*
prototyping, 30
Tabletop Simulator, 133
Takahashi, Kazuki, 9–10
TCG, *see* trading card games (TCGs)
themes, *37*, 59, 62, *67*, 72–73, 116
tournaments/competitions, 6, *25*, 120–123
    esports, 82, 128, 137
    expansions and, 73, 74
    live-service games and, 113, 126, 131
    monetization and, 49
    rules and limits in, 54, 74, 82, *82*, 114–117
    sealed-deck tournaments, 120, 122
    "side decks," 121
trading card games (TCGs), 1–3, *1*, 135–136, *see also Magic: The Gathering; Pokémon the Trading Card Game; Yu-Gi-Oh!*
    CCGs vs., 33–34
    creating card dynamics, 21–23
    customization and perks, 81–82
    design, 15–30
    general structure, 15–18
    how to start building, 29–30
    impact of the digital market, 132–133
    influence on game design, 77–85
    low-number-design philosophy, 18–20
    major names of, 5–13
    manufacturing and distribution, *18*, 56–58, 67, 120
    market for, 129–133
    monetization and logistics of, 56–58
    pros and cons of making, 129–132
    the secondhand market, 55–56
    today's TCGs, 12–13
Turtle Rock Studios, 84

U

user interfaces (UIs), 23, 31, 60, 62, 127–128, 138

V

Valve, 44–45, *see also Artifact*
Vault of the Void, *111*

W

Warcraft, 35
Warhammer franchise, *114*, 114
weather systems, 66, *92*, 107–108, *107*
Whalen, Peter, 77
Witcher 3: Wild Hunt, The, 39–40, *see also* Gwent
Wizards of the Coast, 5–6, 8, 12, *see also Magic: The Gathering*

X

XCOM 2, 19–20, *20*

Y

Yu-Gi-Oh!, 9–12, *10*, *11*, 16, 19, 49

banned cards, 103
booster boxes, 52–53, *52*
card balance issues, *73*
card cost during play, *93*, 95, 99
colors in, 60
compared to other TCGs, 10
Exodia cards' popularity, 105, *106*
expansions and advanced card types, 66, *66*
number of different cards in, 113
"speed duel" format, *121*, 121
starter packs and premade decks, *28*
"trap" cards in, 10, 12, 16–17, 35, 99
Yu-Gi-Oh! Master Duel, 9–10, *11*, *22*, 133

9781032370705